CAMPAIGN • 227

LONDON 1917–18

The bomber blitz

IAN CASTLE

ILLUSTRATED BY CHRISTA HOOK

Series editor Marcus Cowper

First published in Great Britain in 2010 by Osprey Publishing,
Midland House, West Way, Botley, Oxford OX2 0PH, UK
44-02 23rd St, Suite 219, Long Island City, NY 11101, USA

E-mail: info@ospreypublishing.com

A CIP catalogue record for this book is available from the British Library.

ISBN: 978 1 84603 682 8
E-book ISBN: 978 1 84908 299 0

Editorial by Ilios Publishing Ltd, Oxford, UK (www.iliospublishing.com)
Page layout by: The Black Spot
Index by Sandra Shotter
Typeset in Sabon and Myriad Pro
Maps by Bounford.com
Battlescene illustrations by Christa Hook
Originated by PDQ Media
Printed in China through Worldprint Ltd

10 11 12 13 14   10 9 8 7 6 5 4 3 2 1

Osprey Publishing is supporting the Woodland Trust, the UK's leading
woodland conservation charity by funding the dedication of trees.

www.ospreypublishing.com

DEDICATION

Dedicated to the memory of William 'Bill' Stone (1900–2009), Henry
Allingham (1896–2009) and Henry 'Harry' Patch (1898–2009), the last three
surviving UK-based veterans of World War I who all passed away during the
preparation of this book.

ACKNOWLEDGEMENTS

I would like to express my thanks to a number of individuals who have
contributed to this project. As ever Colin Ablett has been most generous
with access to his extensive library, and thanks are due to Claire Frankland
of the Museum of London Docklands and Caroline Brick of the London
Transport Museum for answering my tricky questions. I would also like to
thank Martin Worel in Austria for his help with German translations and
Marton Szigeti in Germany whose great knowledge of the 'Giant' bombers
proved invaluable. And for the colour artwork that illustrates this book I
must express my gratitude to the artist, Christa Hook, who has translated
my simple ideas and thoughts into beautiful works of art.

Unless otherwise stated all photographs used in this book are from my
own collection.

ARTIST'S NOTE

Readers may care to note that the original paintings from which the
colour plates in this book were prepared are available for private sale.
The Publishers retain all reproduction copyright whatsoever. All enquiries
should be addressed to:

Scorpio Gallery, PO Box 475, Hailsham, East Sussex BN27 2SL, UK

The Publishers regret that they can enter into no correspondence upon
this matter.

IMPERIAL WAR MUSEUM COLLECTIONS

Some of the photos in this book come from the Imperial War Museum's
huge collections which cover all aspects of conflict involving Britain
and the Commonwealth since the start of the twentieth century.
These rich resources are available online to search, browse and buy at
www.iwmcollections.org.uk. In addition to Collections Online, you can
visit the Visitor Rooms where you can explore over 8 million photographs,
thousands of hours of moving images, the largest sound archive of its
kind in the world, thousands of diaries and letters written by people in
wartime, and a huge reference library. To make an appointment, call
(020) 7416 5320, or e-mail mail@iwm.org.uk.

Imperial War Museum www.iwm.org.uk

CONTENTS

INTRODUCTION

On the night of 1 October 1916 a lone Zeppelin cautiously approached London from the north. Kapitänleutnant Heinrich Mathy, the most successful of the Zeppelin commanders, steered his ship, *L.31*, stealthily towards the capital, hoping to avoid the gun defences that lay across his path. Just as he approached Cheshunt a searchlight pierced the blackness and illuminated the great bulk of the monstrous raider. More searchlights locked on and within minutes anti-aircraft guns began barking their defiance into the sky. Attracted by the blast of the guns and the flash of their exploding shells, a number of Home Defence pilots patrolling the approaches to London turned to investigate. Swooping into the attack in his BE2c, 2nd Lieutenant Wulstan Tempest launched two unsuccessful attacks, but after his third *L.31* glowed 'red inside like an enormous Chinese lantern and then a flame shot out'. It was the end. *L.31* crashed to earth at Potters Bar in Hertfordshire, the press relishing the fact that the burning wreckage fell, impaled on a stout English oak.

At the beginning of the war the threat posed by Germany's airship fleet caused great concern and for the first 18 months of the conflict Britain had little in the way of an effective response. But the introduction of explosive and incendiary bullets, capable of igniting the highly inflammable hydrogen lifting gas, turned the tide and the destruction of *L.31* had been Germany's fourth

The tangled wreckage of Zeppelin *L.31* at Potters Bar, Hertfordshire, on the morning of 2 October 1916. This fourth loss in the space of a month spelt the end of the Zeppelin threat to London.

loss in the space of a month. Although the British authorities could not know it at the time, the threat of Zeppelin raids on London was over. (For details of Germany's airship offensive against London see Osprey Campaign 193: *London 1914-17: The Zeppelin Menace.*)

However, the effect on morale of bombing London remained a great prize for Germany. Despite its losses, their Navy remained committed to the development of airships to counter Britain's improved defences, but the Army, disillusioned, turned its attention to the potential offered by aeroplanes to carry an effective bomb load to London. It was a change of direction that signalled the advent of London's first blitz.

THE ROAD TO WAR

This was not the first time Germany had planned to launch a bomber offensive against London. In the early weeks of the war, as the German Army pushed the Allies back and the 'race to the sea' was under way, Wilhelm Siegert, commander of the army's Flieger Batallion Nr. 4 proposed the creation of a force to open a strategic bombing campaign against the hub of the British Empire and seat of its government. The limited range of the aircraft available at that time meant any bombing unit required a base close to the French coastal port of Calais, which offered the shortest route to London. Confident of reaching that goal the Oberste Heeresleitung (Army High Command, OHL) approved the creation of a force for the task, allowing Siegert to select the best pilots and observers, and within a few weeks they were formed at an airfield about 10km (6 miles) south of Ostend, at Ghistelles (Gistel) in occupied Belgium. Formed under the name, Fliegerkorps der Obersten Heeresleitung, this highly secret unit adopted the unlikely code-name Brieftauben Abteilung Ostende – the Ostend Carrier Pigeon Detachment – to disguise its identity. But when, in November 1914, the German advance was brought to a halt with Calais out of reach, Siegert's plan was shelved but not forgotten, for plans were already progressing to build new longer-range aircraft – the *Grosskampfflugzeug* (large battle aeroplane) series, the G-type – capable of reaching London from bases in Belgium.

The activities of the Ostend squadron refocused on targets closer at hand, bombing targets behind the Allied lines, until the spring of 1915 when it briefly redeployed to the Eastern Front before returning in July 1915. In December the squadron became Kampfgeschwader 1 der OHL – Battle Squadron 1 of the Army High Command – generally abbreviated to Kagohl 1. For the next eight months Kagohl 1 flew bombing missions, reconnaissance patrols and escort duties over Verdun and later the Somme until, in August 1916, its six *Kampfstaffeln* (flights) – abbreviated to *Kasta* – were split into two separate

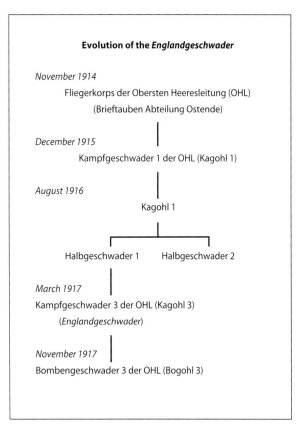

Evolution of the *Englandgeschwader*

November 1914
Fliegerkorps der Obersten Heeresleitung (OHL)
(Brieftauben Abteilung Ostende)

December 1915
Kampfgeschwader 1 der OHL (Kagohl 1)

August 1916
Kagohl 1

Halbgeschwader 1   Halbgeschwader 2

March 1917
Kampfgeschwader 3 der OHL (Kagohl 3)
(*Englandgeschwader*)

November 1917
Bombengeschwader 3 der OHL (Bogohl 3)

Halbgeschwader (half squadrons). Halbgeschwader 1 remained on the Somme while Halbgeschwader 2 redeployed to the Balkans.

A reorganization of Germany's army air service in late 1916 saw the appointment of Ernst von Hoeppner as its supreme commander. He felt confident that the weapon was now available – G-type bombers – to resurrect plans shelved two years earlier for an aeroplane bombing campaign against London. And the unit selected to carry out this mission – Kampfgeschwader 3 der OHL (Kagohl 3) – he formed from the nucleus of Halbgeschwader 1. His decision came at a point when the German Army had already concluded that increasing Zeppelin losses made further attempts on London by that means impossible, a decision stubbornly rejected by the naval airship authorities. And just at this time, as Germany was planning this new means of striking at the morale of the British population, Britain, convinced that the menace of the Zeppelin raids was over, began reducing its home defences to support the growing demands for manpower on the Western Front and in other theatres. A few months later, largely unopposed, German bombers were flying over the streets of London in broad daylight trailing death and destruction in their wake.

CHRONOLOGY

1917

5 March	Hauptmann Ernst Brandenburg appointed commander of Kagohl 3 (*Englandgeschwader*).
25 May	First attempted daylight raid on London, redirected on Folkestone.
5 June	Daylight raid on Sheerness and Shoeburyness. First Gotha shot down.
13 June	First daylight raid on London by Gotha bombers. Highest casualties from a single raid (162 killed, 426 injured).
19 June	Brandenburg injured in crash resulting in amputation of a leg.
23 June	Hauptmann Rudolph Kleine appointed commander of Kagohl 3.
7 July	Second and final daylight raid on London.
19 July	Release of first part of Smuts' report on Home Defence.
8 August	Major-General Ashmore appointed commander of LADA.
17 August	Release of second part of Smuts' report, recommending creation of a single air service.
28 August	Home Defence Group upgraded to Home Defence Brigade.
4/5 September	First night-time raid on London.
6 September	Smuts' report on night raids.
22 September	Arrival of Rfa 501 in Belgium flying R-type 'Giants'.
24 September	Beginning of Harvest Moon Offensive. The first of five raids on London in eight days.
29 September	First London raid involving both Gotha and 'Giant' aircraft.

1/2 October	Last raid of Harvest Moon Offensive.
31 October/ 1 November	Seventh night raid on London.
December	Kagohl 3 re-designated Bogohl 3.
6 December	Eighth night raid on London.
12 December	Rudolph Kleine killed in action. Temporary command of Bogohl 3 passes to Oberleutnant Richard Walter.
18 December	Ninth night raid on London. Highest material damage inflicted in an aeroplane raid (£225,000).

1918

January	Britain establishes an Air Ministry.
28/29 January	Tenth night raid on London. A bomb in Long Acre causes the most casualties in the capital inflicted by a single bomb (38 killed, 85 injured).
29/30 January	Eleventh night raid.
February	Ernst Brandenburg returns to command of Bogohl 3.
16 February	Twelfth night raid. First 1,000kg bomb dropped on London.
17 February	Thirteenth night raid on London – carried out by a single 'Giant'.
7/8 March	Fourteenth night raid on London.
1 April	Formation of the Royal Air Force.
19/20 May	Fifteenth night raid on London – the Whitsun Raid. Largest and final raid of the war (total: two day and 15 night raids).

OPPOSING COMMANDERS

GERMAN COMMANDERS

Generalleutnant Ernst Wilhelm von Hoeppner

Born in January 1860, Ernst Wilhelm von Hoeppner joined the army as a junior officer in a dragoon regiment in 1879 at the beginning of an impressive military career that saw him hold a number of high-profile regimental, field and staff commands. At the outbreak of war in 1914 Hoeppner was chief of the general staff of III Armee, and over the next two years he held various other senior field and staff commands. Then, the OHL, having emerged battered from the maelstrom of the Verdun and Somme campaigns, decided that the *Fliegertruppen* – the army aviation arm – needed re-forming under a general officer with command over all aspects of army aviation. The outcome was the creation of the Luftstreitkräfte and, on the recommendation of Erich Ludendorff, Generalquartiermeister of the German Army, Hoeppner, with no aviation background, was appointed Kommandierender General der Luftstreitkräfte – conveniently abbreviated to Kogenluft – on 12 November 1916.

Kogenluft Ernst Wilhelm von Hoeppner (left) meeting one of his airmen. His decision to end the Army Zeppelin raids on London opened the way for the launch of Operation *Türkenkreuz,* the Gotha bomber raids on the city.

Warming to his new role, shortly after his appointment, Hoeppner issued a memorandum. It stated that he considered airship raids on London no longer viable and as such he planned to open bombing raids against the city with aeroplanes as soon as possible. The aims of such raids were to strike at the morale of the British population, the disruption of war industry and communications, and to impede the cross-Channel supply routes. He stated – a little optimistically – that the G-type bomber aircraft were ready and soon the massive R-type would join them. However, he ended his memorandum on a cautionary note. He stated that raids by the G-type aircraft '... can only succeed provided every detail is carefully prepared, the crews are practised in long-distance overseas flight and the squadron is made up of especially-good aeroplane crews. Any negligence and undue haste will only entail heavy losses for us, and defeat our ends.'

The man given the task of carrying out these orders was Ernst Brandenburg.

Hauptmann Ernst Brandenburg

Born in West Prussia in June 1883, Brandenburg joined the infantry as a young man, becoming a *Leutnant* in 1908. Three years later he attended an aviation training course before returning to his regiment, 6. Westpreussischen Infanterie-Regiment Nr. 149, with whom he went to war in 1914. Promoted to *Hauptmann* in November 1914, Brandenburg received a severe wound the following year

Hauptmann Ernst Brandenburg. Personally selected for the task by Hoeppner, he became commander of Kagohl 3, the *Englandgeschwader*, in March 1917. Brandenburg's calm and calculating manner made him an ideal choice. (C. Ablett)

while serving in the trenches. After his recovery, in November 1915, like so many other soldiers no longer fit to return to the front line, he joined the army's air service. He adapted well to his new role as an observer, flying in two-seater aircraft over the front line and his abilities as an organizer and administrator shone through, quickly bringing him to the attention of his superiors. Following his appointment as Kogenluft in late 1916, Hoeppner personally selected Brandenburg to command the squadron destined to lead the strategic air campaign against London – Kagohl 3. He took up his new command on 5 March 1917, aged 33, and started with a blank piece of paper; there were no guidelines. Brandenburg created an intensive training programme for the crews that would form his squadron; he sent his crews to learn the skills needed for navigation over large expanses of open sea, while the technicalities of formation flying, a tactic considered necessary for the defensive strength of the raiding squadron over hostile territory, were absorbed. Brandenburg also insisted that all aircraft allocated to his squadron were test-flown for at least 25 hours and that his crews all carried out 20 landings, half in daylight and half after dark. Finally, in May 1917, Brandenburg was ready to lead his squadron – now unofficially known as the *Englandgeschwader* (England squadron) – into battle.

Hauptmann Richard von Bentivegni

Born in Rendsburg in Schleswig-Holstein in August 1889, Bentivegni joined the army in March 1905, in 8. Thüringisches Infanterie-Regiment Nr. 153. In August 1906, two days before his 17th birthday he became a *Leutnant* and remained so until he volunteered to join the *Schutztruppe* in German East Africa in 1911. He returned to his regiment at the beginning of August 1914 when he became a company commander, then, in November 1914, while serving on the Western Front, he received promotion to *Oberleutnant*. However, in September 1915 he transferred to Flieger Ersatz Abteilung Nr. 9 at Darmstadt where he trained as an airman. He completed training in December 1915 and moved to Armeeflugpark Nr. 13 where he awaited an active appointment. Then, in January 1916 he joined Feldflieger Abteilung Nr. 28 at the front. Two months later he was promoted to *Hauptmann* and then, in September 1915, transferred to the Reisenflieger Abteilung to train on the giant R-type aircraft before joining Riesenflugzeug Abteilung (Rfa) 501 on the Eastern Front in October 1916, becoming commander of the squadron the following month. In July 1917 Rfa 501 relocated to Berlin where it trained on the new Staaken R.VI 'Giant' before arriving in Belgium in September 1917, when Bentivegni prepared to join the *Englandgeschwader* in the air assault on London.

BRITISH COMMANDERS

Major-General Edward Ashmore

Edward Bailey Ashmore, born in London in 1872, joined the Royal Artillery in 1891, having passed through the Royal Military Academy. Having seen action in the Anglo-Boer War, Ashmore attended Staff College before joining the general staff in 1908. An interest in aviation saw him take flying lessons in 1912 and, after passing the course at the RFC's Central Flying School, he joined the reserve of the RFC in January 1913. As a staff officer with the RFC when war broke out the following year, Ashmore held a home administrative posting before taking command of 5th Wing based at Gosport in April 1915. Four months later he found himself in France in command of 1st Wing followed by command of 1st Brigade, RFC, then later 4th Brigade, during the Somme campaign. At the end of 1916 Ashmore returned to his roots, transferring back to the Royal Artillery.

Following the poor showing offered up by the home defences during the daylight raids on London in the summer of 1917, an official review took steps towards revitalizing London's defences. One of its recommendations called for 'a senior officer of first-rate ability and practical air experience' to command the whole defence of London: aircraft, anti-aircraft guns, searchlights and observation posts.

Ashmore, described as 'a brilliant combination of airman and artillery officer' fitted the bill perfectly. Recalled from Flanders, where he commanded the artillery of 29th Division, he became commander of the newly created London Air Defence Area (LADA) on 5 August 1917. He later commented sardonically, 'The fact that I was exchanging the comparative safety of the Front for the probability of being hanged in the streets of London did not worry me.'

Lieutenant-Colonel Thomas Charles Reginald Higgins

Thomas Higgins, born in Buckinghamshire in July 1880, attended Dartmouth Naval College before joining HMS *Camperdown* as a midshipman in 1897. However, in 1900 Higgins transferred to the Army, serving as a lieutenant in the King's Own Royal Regiment in the Anglo-Boer War. He went on to serve in Nigeria with the West African Frontier Force, 1904–13, during which time, in 1911, he was one of an early batch of army officers to gain his flying certificate. Higgins applied to join the RFC shortly after its formation, but with the officer complement full, he found himself fighting in France until wounded early in the war.

In 1915 Higgins did transfer to the RFC, quickly becoming a flight commander before his appointment as commander of the newly created No. 19 Reserve Aeroplane Squadron in England in February 1916, with responsibility for all the widely distributed aircraft committed to the defence of London. In April 1916 the squadron was renamed No. 39 (Home Defence) squadron, which he commanded until June 1916 when he became Inspector of Home

Defence. Then, in February 1917, with the rank of lieutenant-colonel, Higgins took command of Home Defence Wing which became Home Defence Group (11 squadrons and one depot squadron) in March 1917. Later, as the Home Defence organization expanded in response to the German bomber offensive, the group reorganized as Home Defence Brigade (14 squadrons and one depot squadron) and eventually became VI Brigade in October 1917.

Lieutenant-Colonel Maximilian St Leger Simon

Simon, the son of a physician/surgeon, was born in Malacca, Straits Settlement (now Malaysia), in 1876 and entered the Royal Military Academy in 1893. Two years later he received a commission in the Royal Engineers where he specialized in submarine mining and studied coastal searchlights. He served in Singapore, England and Canada before returning to England in 1910. The following year Simon became a staff officer at the War Office where he remained until he received a brevet lieutenant-colonelcy in late 1915 and headed for France with the 197th (Land Drainage) Company, RE. Then, in February 1916, when the War Office took over responsibility for London's defence from the Admiralty, they recalled Simon and placed him in a position to supervise the construction of gun and searchlight positions around the city. Later, in December 1916, he became Anti-Aircraft Defence Commander, London.

OPPOSING PLANS

GERMAN PLANS

With the appointment of Hoeppner as Kogenluft in November 1916, the plan to commence an aeroplane bombing campaign began to take shape, based on the new G-type *Grosskampfflugzeug* (large battle aeroplane) series. In September 1916 the Gothaer Waggonfabrik AG, formerly a builder of railway carriages, received approval for production to commence on their latest aircraft design, the G.IV. Developed from the earlier G.II and G.III, the G.IV, generally known as the Gotha, was the aircraft the army had been waiting for.

Powered by two 260hp Mercedes engines, the Gotha G.IV could maintain a speed of 80mph (130kmph) in favourable conditions with an impressive ceiling of around 18,000ft (5,500m). Despite its uncomfortable open cockpits and 78ft (24m) wingspan, it flew well, was manoeuvrable and could carry a bomb load of between 300 and 400kg and two 7.92mm Parabellum machine guns for defence. And most importantly, it had the range to reach London and return to bases in occupied Belgium. Its weak point was its instability when coming in to land without the ballast of bombs and fuel.

The three-man crew consisted of the commander, pilot and rear-gunner. The commander, an officer, occupied the front nose position. He was responsible for navigation and acted as observer, bomb-aimer and front-gunner. The pilot could be either an officer or senior NCO, while the rear-gunner was often a junior NCO. An innovation on the G.IV was a slanting 'tunnel' built through the fuselage, which gave the rear-gunner the added advantage of being able to fire downwards at attacking aircraft taking advantage of the traditional blind spot below the tail.

Initially the load of the Gotha G.IV in the daylight raids on London consisted of a mixture of 50kg explosive bombs and 12.5kg explosive or incendiary bombs. The larger bomb was about 5ft (1.5m) long and 7in. (18cm) in diameter and either armed for detonation on impact or with a delay fuse which allowed the bomb to penetrate through a building

A view of a Gotha pilot's cockpit and the forward gun position occupied by the aircraft commander. The passage to the right of the pilot allowed the commander to move within the aircraft.

A British aerial reconnaissance photo of the Kagohl 3 airfield at Sint-Denijs-Westrem, the home airfield for Staffeln 13 and 14. Later, in September 1917, the 'Giants' of Rfa 501 shared the airfield.

before exploding. However, estimates indicate that up to a third of 50kg bombs failed to explode and another 10 per cent detonated in mid-air. The actual bomb load varied but on the early daylight raids a typical load of 300kg would be four 50kg and eight 12.5kg bombs. Later in the campaign the Gothas mainly utilized the 50kg explosive bomb with a limited number of the 100kg type, as well as incendiaries.

When he first took office, Hoeppner anticipated that 30 Gotha G.IVs would be available to begin attacks on London by 1 February 1917 and he further noted that development of the *Riesenflugzeug* (giant aeroplane), or the R-type, was progressing well, anticipating that these even larger and more powerful aircraft would soon be added to the weapons at his disposal.

Halbgeschwader 1 returned to Ghistelles and reformed as Kagohl 3. The three existing Kasta 1, 4 and 6, became Kasta 13, 14 and 15 of the new squadron and were boosted by three more; Kasta 16 joined immediately, 17 and 18 in place by July 1917. Each *Kasta* consisted of six aircraft, giving a squadron strength of 36 aircraft, plus three allocated to the HQ. New airfields were under construction for the squadron around Ghent. But there were delays; the first airfields, Melle-Gontrode and Sint-Denijs-Westrem, were not ready until April 1917, followed in July by Mariakerke and Oostakker.

Although anticipated in February the first of the squadron's aircraft did not arrive at Ghistelles until March 1917. The following month Kasta 13 and 14 transferred to their new airfield at Sint-Denijs-Westrem, while Kasta 15 and 16, along with the HQ, moved to Melle-Gontrode. Yet Kagohl 3 was still not ready to begin its work. Throughout the training period the crews experienced engine problems with their new aircraft, requiring the rest of April to improve though not completely rectify these problems. And then there was the fuel issue. Tests proved that the engines would consume their full capacity of 175 gallons (800 litres) of petrol on even the most direct return flight to London. Any deviation or evasion tactics would exhaust the onboard supply and imperil a safe return. Therefore reserve fuel tanks were authorized for all the squadron's aircraft, their fitting causing further delay.

British and German airfields actively engaged in the raids, 1917

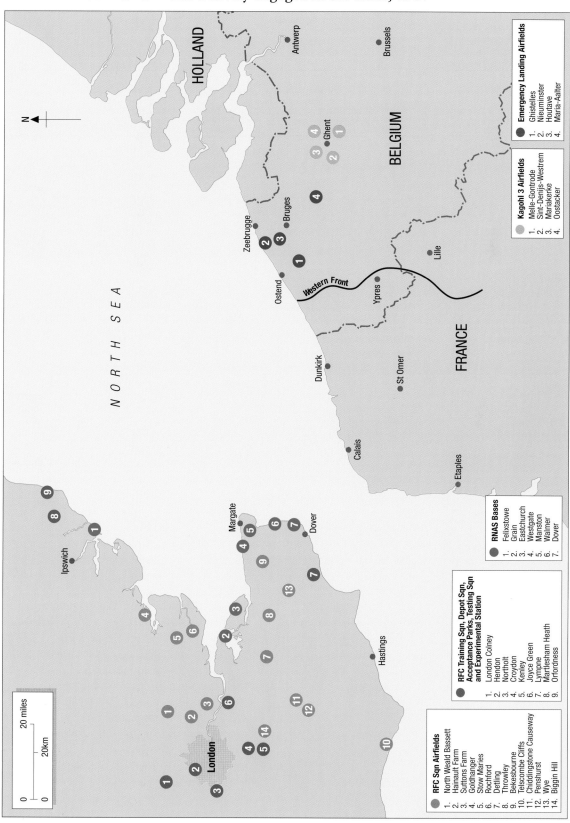

N

HOLLAND

BELGIUM

FRANCE

NORTH SEA

Antwerp

Brussels

Ghent

Bruges

Zeebrugge

Ostend

Lille

Ypres

Western Front

Dunkirk

St Omer

Calais

Etaples

Margate

Dover

Ipswich

Hastings

London

Emergency Landing Airfields
1. Ghistelles
2. Nieuminster
3. Houtave
4. Maria-Aalter

Kagohl 3 Airfields
1. Melle-Gontrode
2. Sint-Denijs-Westrem
3. Mariakerke
4. Oostacker

RNAS Bases
1. Felixstowe
2. Grain
3. Eastchurch
4. Westgate
5. Manston
6. Walmer
7. Dover

**RFC Training Sqn, Depot Sqn,
Acceptance Parks, Testing Sqn
and Experimental Station**
1. London Colney
2. Hendon
3. Northolt
4. Croydon
5. Kenley
6. Joyce Green
7. Lympne
8. Martlesham Heath
9. Orfordness

RFC Sqn Airfields
1. North Weald Bassett
2. Hainault Farm
3. Suttons Farm
4. Goldhanger
5. Stow Maries
6. Rochford
7. Detling
8. Throwley
9. Bekesbourne
10. Telscombe Cliffs
11. Chiddingstone Causeway
12. Penshurst
13. Wye
14. Biggin Hill

20 miles

20km

15

But by mid-May Brandenburg announced that his squadron was ready to make its first attack on London. There were ongoing delays fitting the reserve fuel tanks but he reasoned that a refuelling stop near the coast would allow the topping up of the existing tanks thus granting a little leeway. So all was ready, the crews of the *Englandgeschwader* now just waited impatiently for the advent of good weather before launching Operation *Türkenkreuz* (*Turk's Cross*) – the code-name for the attack on London.

BRITISH PLANS

Lieutenant-General David Henderson, commander of the Royal Flying Corps. With the apparent removal of the aerial threat to Britain following Zeppelin losses in autumn 1916, Henderson drew heavily on the Home Defence squadrons to boost his squadrons on the Western Front.

There was a genuine belief in Britain that, after the successes against Zeppelin raiders in the autumn of 1916, the aerial threat was over. Even an audacious raid by a single aeroplane on south-west London on 28 November failed to cause any undue concern amongst the military. Largely unobserved it dropped six bombs between Brompton Road and Victoria in full daylight, causing only minor damage and little comment, but the press issued a cautionary warning about future aeroplane attacks. But when no more Zeppelins – or aeroplanes – appeared over the capital for the rest of 1916 or in the early weeks of 1917, the fear of aerial raids largely evaporated.

At the opening of 1917 the home defences were those instigated and developed since the War Office took over the responsibility for the defence of London from the Admiralty in February 1916. It was a defence system designed to oppose the night-time raids by German airships. The Home Defence Wing of the Royal Flying Corps (RFC) contained 11 squadrons assigned to the defence of Britain, of which four defended the approaches to London: Nos. 37, 39, 50 and 78. The four 'London' squadrons each had an establishment of 24 aircraft, the rest set at 18. However, as a snapshot, a report dated 7 March 1917 showed that the 'London' squadrons could muster only 64 aircraft out of an establishment of 96, and ten of those were undergoing repairs. And because of the nature of night-time defence against airships, the aircraft allocated to these squadrons were older, slower, more stable aircraft, such as the BE2c, BE12 and FE2b. The tactics were simple; each aircraft operated individually, flying along pre-set patrol lines hunting for Zeppelins caught in searchlights as they approached the city. The aircraft did not carry radios as the Admiralty opposed their introduction claiming they would interfere with Navy signals. It was one of many flashpoints between the Admiralty and the War Office in their troubled relationship in the field of aviation.

However, stretched as the Home Defence squadrons were, with the diminishing threat from enemy airships and an ever-growing demand for aircraft and personnel on the Western Front, moves were afoot to reduce the number even more. Early in February 1917, Lieutenant-General David Henderson, commander of the RFC, advised that he urgently required two new night-flying squadrons for service in France. While the aircraft would be available at the beginning of March, Henderson now asked for the transfer of 36 trained pilots from the Home Defence squadrons to fly them, with an additional nine pilots each month as replacements, adding that, 'the diminished risk from Zeppelin attack amply justifies this temporary reduction'. Three days later the War Cabinet approved the transfer.

Control of the anti-aircraft gun defences of London had rested with Lt. Col. M. St L. Simon, RE, from December 1916. Almost immediately Simon found his command reduced. The plan of his predecessor, Admiral Sir Percy Scott, included two gun rings around London, one 5 miles (8km) out and the other 9 miles (14km) from the centre, each gun position mounted with twin guns, supported by an outer ring of searchlights. The plan required 84 guns in 42 gun-positions, but in January 1917 cuts reduced the total available to 65 following the Admiralty's demand for guns to arm merchant ships in the battle against the German U-boats. As a result Simon abandoned the original plan. Only three double-gun stations remained, the other 39 downgraded to single-gun positions and the remaining 20 guns relocated to bolster the defences on north and eastern approaches to the capital.

And then one final dramatic decision reduced London's effective defence further. At a high-ranking meeting on 6 March 1917, attention focused on further Home Defence cuts to allow redeployment of manpower to the Western Front. Field Marshal Lord French, commander-in-chief of British Home Forces, then made a remarkable recommendation, one that received immediate approval: 'No aeroplanes or seaplanes, even if recognized as hostile, will be fired at, either by day or night, except by those anti-aircraft guns situated near the Restricted Coast Area which are specially detailed for the purpose.'

With AA guns no longer on 24-hour alert, big reductions in manning levels followed. However, Lt. Col. Simon, who had been working on a plan to oppose future aeroplane attacks, remained unconvinced about the end of the aerial threat and, without official approval, completed his defence plan before filing it away for possible future use.

It was against this scaled-down defence system that the *Englandgeschwader* was about to open its campaign.

In December 1915, replaced as commander of the BEF, Field Marshal Lord French returned to Britain as commander-in-chief, British Home Forces. He presided over the gradual reduction in Britain's aerial defence capability, which left it exposed when Germany began aeroplane raids in 1917.

THE 1917 RAIDS

THE CAMPAIGN BEGINS

Having informed Hoeppner in mid-May that he was ready to launch his first attack on London, Brandenburg then faced the frustration of a period of bad weather which prevented his carrying out the plan. In fact the British weather, which had proved an implacable opponent to the Zeppelin raids, continued to dog the bomber raids too. Weather forecasting in the early years of the 20th century was simplistic in comparison with modern satellite systems, and in 1917 weather systems approaching Britain over the Atlantic remained unknown to German forces. Good weather, wind speeds and directions over the North Sea could be predicted with some accuracy, but what was to come over England could not.

In fact, before Brandenburg could launch his first raid, an audacious attack by a single Albatross C VII of Feldflieger Abteilung Nr. 19 on the night of 6/7 May did reach London. The crew dropped five 10kg bombs between Hackney and Holloway, killing one man and causing two injuries, before returning unmolested to Belgium. However, on 24 May 1917, Brandenburg received a positive forecast for the following day and with that he issued orders for the first bomber squadron raid on London. Twenty-three Gotha G.IVs set

Gotha G.IV aircraft of Kagohl 3 preparing for a raid on England in 1917. Bad weather caused Brandenburg to abort the first two planned raids on London, but the third, on 13 June, delivered a devastating blow against the city. (C. Ablett)

off for London, but thick cloud cover blanketing the city forced Brandenburg to turn away and head home via secondary targets in Kent. The bombs intended for London caused casualties of an unprecedented level, mainly on the unsuspecting population of Folkestone and the military camp at Shorncliffe; 95 were killed and 195 injured. The defensive response was confused, uncoordinated and ineffective. Only specified coastal anti-aircraft batteries opened fire – as ordered on 7 March – and despite over 70 aircraft taking to the air, only one got close enough to engage. The stiffest opposition came from Royal Naval Air Service (RNAS) aircraft based in the Dunkirk area who encountered the returning raiders and claimed one Gotha shot down over the sea while another crashed on landing near Bruges, killing the crew.

The raid caused a public outcry. Makeshift arrangements called for training squadrons, aircraft acceptance parks and experimental stations to make aircraft available for patrols and another 20 aircraft were drafted into the Home Defence squadrons. A conference then followed to 'report upon the defence of the United Kingdom against attack by aeroplanes', yet it achieved little. To speed up the transmission of accurate information, 24 trained anti-aircraft observers were withdrawn from France and redeployed on lightships anchored in the approaches to the Thames estuary, but other than that it was felt anything else would have a detrimental effect on front-line aircraft requirements. The question of fitting wireless transmitters into RFC aircraft again foundered in the face of Admiralty opposition. Inconclusive discussions also took place at the conference about the practicality of a public air raid warning system.

A second raid followed on 5 June with similar results. Weather conditions forced Brandenburg to turn away and head for secondary targets along the Thames estuary. His bombs were hitting home as Home Defence pilots still struggled up to operational height. There was however one beacon of light for the defenders; the eight coastal AA guns around Shoeburyness and Sheerness opened on the raiders and brought down one of the Gothas which crashed into the estuary. Then, three days later, on 7 June, an order cancelled the three-month-old restriction on general anti-aircraft fire. Lieutenant-Colonel Simon immediately dusted off his plan, pigeon-holed since March, and prepared for the inevitable raid on London that everyone knew must follow. It came on the morning of Wednesday 13 June.

LONDON'S FIRST DAYTIME RAID

With a good forecast from his weather officer, Brandenburg prepared his crews for a third attempt on London. All aircraft now had the reserve fuel tanks fitted so it would be a direct flight – he chose a morning departure as there was a possibility of thunderstorms later. On 13 June, 20 aircraft took off from the two airfields near Ghent, but very quickly two turned back with engine problems. The rest continued on course; the mood was buoyant. One later wrote, 'We can recognise the men in the machine flying nearest us, and signals and greetings are exchanged. A feeling of absolute security and indomitable confidence in our success are our predominant emotions.'

Shortly after, one Gotha left the formation and turned southwards towards the Kent coastal town of Margate on which it dropped five bombs; moments later it was gone. Word of the raid reached Home Forces GHQ, followed swiftly by news of a large formation of aircraft approaching the Essex coast. At this point three more Gothas left the formation, two peeling off towards

Shoeburyness, where they dropped six bombs before heading home while the other crossed to the south of the Thames and followed a course towards Greenwich, believed to be on a photo-reconnaissance mission. Brandenburg continued towards London with the remaining 14 aircraft in two formations flying abreast on a wide front. The noise they created was so great that those on the ground claimed they heard it ten minutes before the aircraft came into view. Yet most who came out into their gardens on this warm, hazy, summer's morning to watch these 'silver specks' flying overhead, presumed them to be friendly aircraft and watched them pass in admiration.

News of the approach of the Gothas reached Nos. 37, 39 and 50 squadrons at 10.53am. Twenty minutes later the additional formations instructed to assist in defence received orders to take off. At 11.24am the 3in. 20cwt AA gun at Romford became the first of the London guns to open fire, followed by the Rainham gun at 11.30am – but others struggled to locate the target in the hazy sky. One of the Gotha commanders described the moment: 'Suddenly there stand, as if by magic here and there in our course, little clouds of cotton, the greetings of enemy guns. They multiply with astonishing rapidity. We fly through them and leave the suburbs behind us. It is the heart of London that must be hit.'

Moments later the first bomb dropped, harmlessly, on an allotment in North Street, Barking, immediately followed by another seven that fell in East Ham. Two in Alexandra Road damaged 42 houses, killing four and injuring 11. Another bomb fell on the Royal Albert Docks where it killed eight dockworkers and damaged buildings, vehicles and a railway truck.

The City of London was now clearly in view directly ahead and Kagohl 3 closed up into a wide-diamond formation. One of the commanders looked out entranced as though a tourist, 'We see the bridges, the Tower of London, Liverpool [Street] Station, the Bank of England, the Admiralty's palace – everything sharply outlined in the glaring sunlight'.

At 11.35am, over Regent's Park, Brandenburg fired a signal flare and the whole formation turned to the east, back towards the City. Once over their target 72 bombs rained down in the space of two minutes within a 1-mile (2km) radius of Liverpool Street Station – stretching from Clerkenwell in the west to Stepney in the east and from Dalston in the north to Bermondsey in the south. Even as the bombs fell people rushed outside or grabbed a vantage point to see this bewildering, confusing spectacle. An American journalist, travelling across the City on a bus observed that,

One of the 47 ceramic plaques in 'Postman's Park', erected to celebrate the heroism of ordinary Londoners. Smith was in Central Street during the raid of 13 June. A number of factory girls rushed from a building where they were working but Smith pushed them back in and pulled the door closed behind them just as a bomb exploded in the street and killed him.

From every office and warehouse and tea shop men and women strangely stood still, gazing up into the air. The conductor mounted the stairs to suggest that outside passengers should seek safety inside. Some of them did so.

'I'm not a religious man,' remarked the conductor, 'but what I say is, we are all in God's hands and if we are going to die we may as well die quiet.'

But some inside passengers were determined that if they had to die quiet they might as well see something first and they climbed on top and with wonderstruck eyes watched the amazing drama of the skies.

Three bombs hit Liverpool Street Station. One fell on the edge of platform no. 9 blasting apart a passenger carriage and causing two others to burn ferociously just as the train was about to depart. A second bomb fell close by, striking carriages used by military doctors. Casualties in the station rapidly mounted to 16 killed and 15 injured. Siegfried Sassoon, the war poet, was at the station that day while on leave and considered, 'In a trench one was acclimatized to the notion of being exterminated and there was a sense of organized retaliation. But here one was helpless; an invisible enemy sent destruction spinning down from a fine weather sky.'

BELOW LEFT
The funeral procession through the East End on 20 June 1917 of the 18 children killed in Poplar at the Upper North Street School. (C. Ablett)

BELOW RIGHT
The monument to those killed at Upper North Street School in Poplar Recreation Ground, paid for by public subscription. The monument bears the names of all 18 victims, the majority of whom were under six years old.

The 13 June 1917 raid

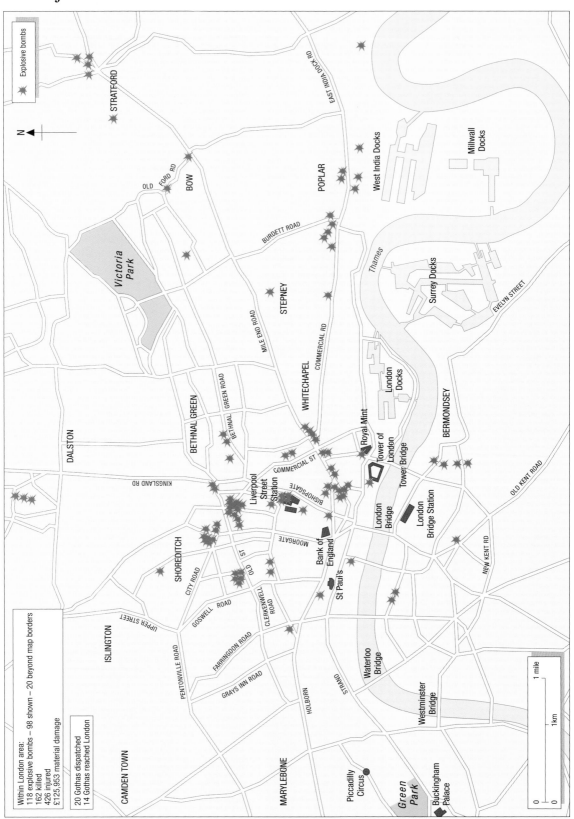

Within London area:
118 explosive bombs – 98 shown – 20 beyond map borders
162 killed
426 injured
£125,953 material damage

20 Gothas dispatched
14 Gothas reached London

Explosive bombs

N

MARYLEBONE

CAMDEN TOWN

ISLINGTON

DALSTON

BETHNAL GREEN

STRATFORD

BOW

Victoria Park

OLD FORD RD

STEPNEY

POPLAR

EAST INDIA DOCK RD

West India Docks

Millwall Docks

BURDETT ROAD

MILE END ROAD

COMMERCIAL RD

WHITECHAPEL

BETHNAL GREEN ROAD

KINGSLAND RD

SHOREDITCH

COMMERCIAL ST

Liverpool Street Station

BISHOPSGATE

OLD ST

CITY ROAD

GOSWELL ROAD

CLERKENWELL ROAD

MOORGATE

Bank of England

Royal Mint

Tower of London

Tower Bridge

London Docks

Thames

Surrey Docks

EVELYN STREET

BERMONDSEY

OLD KENT ROAD

NEW KENT RD

London Bridge

London Bridge Station

St Paul's

UPPER STREET

PENTONVILLE ROAD

FARRINGDON ROAD

GRAYS INN ROAD

HOLBORN

STRAND

Waterloo Bridge

Westminster Bridge

Piccadilly Circus

Green Park

Buckingham Palace

1 mile

1km

0

0

22

Other bombs fell all around. At 65 Fenchurch Street two bombs partially demolished the five-storey office building while claiming 19 lives and injuring another 13. Thomas Burke, working in his third-floor office, heard 'ominous rumbles' and then,

> ... came two deafening crashes. The building swayed and trembled. Two big plate-glass windows came smashing through. Deep fissures appeared in the walls, and I was thrown to my knees.... Looking out of my window on to a street that seemed enveloped by a thick mist... a girl, who had been standing in a doorway of a provision shop, next door, having now lost both her legs... a certified accountant, who had offices near mine, lying dead beside his daughter, who had tried to help him.

Of nine men working on the roof of a brass founders just to the west of Liverpool Street station, eight were killed and, not far away in Central Street, a policeman just prevented a number of female factory workers dashing into the street as a bomb exploded and killed him. Countless other dramatic and tragic stories emerged from the few minutes of horror that descended on London that summer's morning – but there was one above all others that left an indelible mark

Having passed over the city, those aircraft still carrying bombs unloaded them on east London as they departed. Tragically one fell on the Upper North Street School in Poplar. The 50kg bomb smashed through three floors of the building killing two children in its path before exploding on the ground floor in a classroom crammed full with 64 infants. Once the dust and debris had settled rescuers pulled the mangled bodies of 14 children from the wreckage along with 30 more injured by the blast, two of whom later died. Another bomb landed on a school in City Road but failed to detonate.

Yet, as Kagohl 3 completed their mission, they were still largely unmolested. Although some 94 individual defensive sorties were flown by the RFC and RNAS, the time it took to gain the Gotha's operating height, and the short time the enemy formation was over the city meant that only 11 got close enough to the departing raiders to open fire – all without serious effect. One of these, a Bristol Fighter from No. 35 (Training) squadron, finally caught up with three straggling Gothas over Ilford, Essex. Flown by Captain C. W. E. Cole-Hamilton, with Captain C. H. Keevil as observer, it closed to attack but in the exchange that followed a bullet pierced Keevil's neck and killed him. Defenceless, Cole-Hamilton turned sharply away and headed for home. Eleven of the London AA guns opened fire on the raiders but scored no success. All the Gothas returned safely to their bases, having caused £125,953 worth of material damage in London, killing 162 and injuring 426 – this raid inflicting the highest single casualty total of the campaign on the city – and leaving the Home Defence organization exposed and largely powerless in its wake.

REACTION AND RESPONSE

The feeling of outrage amongst the public was great and the clamour for reprisal raids on German towns gained voice. Zeppelins had approached under the cloak of darkness, but the Gothas appeared, brazenly, in broad daylight. In addition, the question of the lack of public air raid warnings was also the subject of much debate – one that the Government struggled to decide upon.

It was clear that being out in the streets during a raid was more dangerous than being under cover, yet when enemy aircraft appeared people ran out into the streets to watch them. Would even more of the curious go into the streets, the Government considered, if they knew a raid was imminent, risking their own safety and hindering the movement of the emergency services?

The following day Brandenburg flew to Germany, ordered to report to Supreme Headquarters to relate the details of the raid to the Kaiser; he received the Pour le Mérite (the 'Blue Max') for his achievement. But on his homeward journey on 19 June disaster struck. The engine of his two-seater Albatross stalled and the aircraft crashed, killing his pilot and, although Brandenburg was dragged alive from the wreckage, it proved necessary to amputate one of his legs. The news stunned the previously jubilant crews of Kagohl 3.

In London the War Cabinet met on the afternoon of the raid and again the following day to consider this new threat. A demand for a dramatic increase in the strength of the RFC was, after discussion, finally approved in July but this was long term. In the meantime, a further meeting already planned for 15 June took place with Field-Marshal Sir Douglas Haig and Major-General Hugh Trenchard present, respectively commanding the Army and RFC on the Western Front. Reluctantly Trenchard approved the temporary detachment of two front-line squadrons to take part in enhanced patrols on each side of the English Channel; No. 56 Squadron (equipped with the SE5a) moved to Bekesbourne near Canterbury and No. 66 Squadron (Sopwith Pups) relocated to Calais. But Trenchard stressed the importance of the return of both squadrons to him by 5 July. Haig needed the RFC at full strength to support his major attack at Ypres, intended to push through and clear the Germans from the Belgian coast.

Meanwhile, Higgins, commanding Home Defence Brigade, RFC, was beginning to receive new, more efficient aircraft for his squadrons, as Sopwith Pups, Sopwith 1½ Strutters, SE5as and Armstrong-Whitworth FK8s joined his roster. This meant that pilots familiar only with the BE types needed a period of retraining. At the same time the RNAS at Eastchurch received a batch of new Sopwith Camels previously earmarked for France. However, Lt. Col. Simon's request for an additional 45 AA guns, to bolster the thin defences on the eastern approaches to the capital and complete his previously shelved plans, failed because neither the guns nor the men to crew them were available. Further meetings also took place regarding the implementation of public air raid warnings but again the Government blocked their introduction – citing this time, amongst other reasons, evidence that munitions workers alerted to air raids had left their work place and often did not return after the threat had passed – having a negative effect on war production.

Back in Belgium a new man arrived at Melle-Gontrode, the headquarters of Kagohl 3. Hauptmann Rudolph Kleine took up his position as Brandenburg's replacement in late June and waited, like his predecessor, for a suitable break in the weather. With no option presenting itself for London, Kleine ordered an attack on the naval town of Harwich on 4 July, which proved successful. By now Trenchard's loan of two squadrons was over. The day after the Harwich raid No. 56 Squadron headed back to France, having, as one of their pilots put it, 'stood by, perfectly idle'. No. 66 Squadron left Calais a day later, and then, inevitably, the day following their departure, Kagohl 3 launched its next attack on London.

THE SECOND DAYLIGHT RAID –
SATURDAY 7 JULY

Kleine chose an early take-off again, and reduced each aircraft's bomb load, to allow his formation to fly faster and higher. Word of the approach of the formation of 22 Gothas, transmitted early by observers on the Kentish Knock lightship, meant that 15 minutes later defence aircraft were taking off, enabling some to engage Kagohl 3 on the way to London. One Gotha wheeled away with engine problems, making a brief bombing run over Margate before heading home. The main body crossed the coastline near the mouth of the river Crouch, flying in close formation at about 12,000ft (3,650m), heading west towards the landmark of Epping Forest before beginning to climb for their bombing run. No. 37 Squadron, directly in the Gotha's flight path, had at least 11 aircraft in the air, but realistically only its four Sopwith Pups could hope to engage the Gothas. Three of them attacked the formation: one pilot gave up his attack when his guns jammed, another suffered engine problems and a third abandoned his attack because of a combination of both.

Other pilots with high-performance aircraft closed to engage but many suffered problems with guns jamming that day. Despite this increased attention and the fire of AA guns along their route, the Gothas continued on their course without significant distraction and, as they got closer to their target, Kleine tightened up the formation. Kleine led, then behind came two flights of eight aircraft, side by side, extended for about a mile, with the remaining four bringing up the rear. Once over Epping Forest, Kleine signalled the formation to begin its turn towards the city.

The morning was bright and sunny with a light haze in the eastern sky. Before the guns opened and the bombs began to drop many onlookers, watching the approaching flight, described it in picturesque terms, likening it to a flock of birds, while a journalist wrote: 'To the spectator, in the midst of a quiet orderly London suburb, busily engaged in its Saturday shopping, it seemed ludicrously incredible that this swarm of black specks moving across the summer sky was a squadron of enemy aircraft, laden with explosive bombs waiting to be dropped into "the brown" of London's vast expanse of brick and mortar.'

Moments later the peace of that Saturday morning was broken. At 10.21am the AA gun at Higham Hill opened fire, followed by Wanstead two minutes

THE FIRST DAYLIGHT RAID, 25 MAY 1917 (pp. 26–27)

Here we see Gotha G.IV 405/16 (1) carrying the markings (2) of Oberleutnant Hans-Ulrich von Trotha, about to take part in the first attempt by Kagohl 3 to bomb London on Friday 25 May 1917. Twenty-three Gotha G.IVs set out for London from their Belgian airfields that day. However, the weather came to London's rescue as thick cloud cover over the city forced the formation to turn away over Tilbury and head home via secondary targets in Kent. The bombs intended for London caused casualties of an unprecedented level, mainly on the unsuspecting population of Folkestone and the military camp at Shorncliffe.

The aircraft shows the standard pale blue finish (3) used on daylight bombing raids, with pale grey engine compartments. Defensive armament consisted of two 7.92mm Parabellum machine guns, one in the front cockpit (4) on a ring mounting and one in the rear (hidden behind rear wing struts). Mesh guards fitted to prevent the rear gunner shooting off the rear-mounted propeller blades resulted in a limited lateral field of fire. The usual bomb load on daylight raids amounted to 300kg;

typically this could be made up with six 50kg bombs or a combination of four 50kg and eight 12.5kg bombs. The 50kg bombs were mounted externally (5), two under the nose and up to four at the junction of wing and fuselage. The smaller bombs, carried in internal racks, dropped through trapdoors.

The senior member of the crew occupied the cockpit in the nose of the Gotha from where he controlled navigation, observation, bomb-aiming and also operated the front machine gun. All of the three-man crew were seated in the open, making long flights uncomfortable and requiring the crew to be well protected from the wind and cold (6).

The Gotha was a reliable aircraft in flight, it had good manoeuvrability and its two 260hp Mercedes engines (7) gave a maximum speed of 87mph. However, the great flaw in the Gotha design was its instability when lightened by the release of its bomb load and consumption of its fuel supply. An extremely high percentage of all Gotha losses resulted from landing accidents on the return from raiding missions.

later. The guns at Palmers Green, Finchley, Highbury and Parliament Hill then opened up too. As the Gothas banked the formation appeared to open out into two groups, that on the left passing south over Tottenham while those to the right continued westwards before turning south-east as they approached Hendon. The first guns of the Western AA district opened fire at 10.26am, the guns at Tower Bridge and Hyde Park joined in at 10.30am. Another journalist takes up the story, '… for five minutes the noise was deafening. Shells bursting in the air left puffs of black smoke, which expanded and drifted into one another. It seemed impossible that the raiders could escape being hit. Machines were often hidden in the smoke, but always they came through safely.'

With the increase in gunfire the Gotha formations opened out and began evasive tactics. The first bomb fell on Chingford, followed by a handful more falling in Tottenham and Edmonton inflicting limited damage to property. Then, in Stoke Newington – the scene of the first London Zeppelin raid – the human tragedies began. Four bombs fell close together, in Cowper Road, Wordsworth Road and two in Boleyn Road. In Cowper and Wordsworth roads the bombs severely damaged three houses and another 60 suffered lesser damage, but the bomb that exploded in Boleyn Road delivered a more deadly effect. William Stanton was in the road when the bomb fell: 'About 10.30am someone shouted in the street, "The Germans!" I looked up and saw the aeroplanes. People were running everywhere. There was a terrible explosion, and a hundred yards away three houses were blown to the ground.'

The explosion killed a 12-year-old grocer's delivery boy as he cycled past and a naturalized German baker and his wife died while working in their shop; seven other lives were lost in the blast and nine injured. Over 50 buildings, many let out as tenements, also suffered damage.

The raiding aircraft continued southwards over Dalston, Hoxton and Shoreditch before reaching the City where they turned to the east and continued bombing as they set course for home. Meanwhile the western part of the

LEFT
Members of the public and a policeman seek shelter during the raid on Saturday 7 July. A newspaper reported that buses stopped while the passengers and crew got off and dashed into buildings before retaking their seats when the Gothas had passed.

RIGHT
Bomb damage caused on 7 July to the German Gymnasium in Pancras Road, between King's Cross and St Pancras stations. Built in 1864–65 by the German Gymnastics Society, it is believed to be the first purpose-built gymnasium in the country.

The 7 July 1917 raid

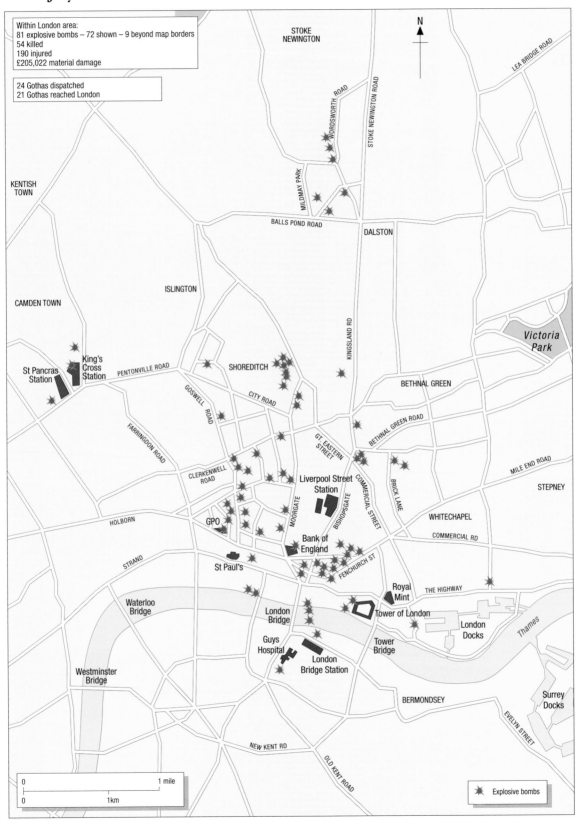

Within London area:
81 explosive bombs – 72 shown – 9 beyond map borders
54 killed
190 injured
£205,022 material damage

24 Gothas dispatched
21 Gothas reached London

N

STOKE NEWINGTON

WORDSWORTH ROAD

STOKE NEWINGTON ROAD

LEA BRIDGE ROAD

MILDMAY PARK

BALLS POND ROAD

DALSTON

KENTISH TOWN

CAMDEN TOWN

ISLINGTON

KINGSLAND RD

Victoria Park

St Pancras Station

King's Cross Station

PENTONVILLE ROAD

SHOREDITCH

CITY ROAD

BETHNAL GREEN

GOSWELL ROAD

FARRINGDON ROAD

CLERKENWELL ROAD

GT EASTERN STREET

BETHNAL GREEN ROAD

MILE END ROAD

STEPNEY

Liverpool Street Station

COMMERCIAL STREET

BRICK LANE

HOLBORN

GPO

MOORGATE

BISHOPSGATE

WHITECHAPEL

COMMERCIAL RD

STRAND

St Paul's

Bank of England

FENCHURCH ST

Royal Mint

THE HIGHWAY

Waterloo Bridge

London Bridge

Tower of London

London Docks

Thames

Westminster Bridge

Guys Hospital

London Bridge Station

Tower Bridge

BERMONDSEY

Surrey Docks

EVELYN STREET

NEW KENT RD

OLD KENT ROAD

0		1 mile

0	1km

Explosive bombs

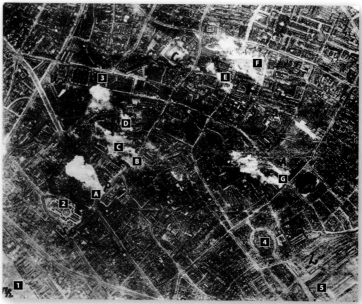

formation was now closing in on the City too. Bombs fell close to King's Cross Station and around Bartholomew Close, Little Britain, Aldersgate Street and Barbican, causing significant destruction, while a number of fires also broke out. One bomb, falling on the roof of the Central Telegraph Office in St Martins Le Grand, caused significant damage to the two top floors of this large building. More bombs fell in and around Fenchurch Street, Leadenhall Street and Billingsgate Fish Market, while another landed in Tower Hill, close to the Tower of London.

The Tower Hill bomb exploded outside offices where some 80 people were sheltering. Those inside heard a deafening crash followed by 'a blinding flash, a chaos of breaking glass' then dust, soot and fumes filled the air. The blast killed eight and injured 15 of those taking shelter, while outside, the explosion left 'three horses lying badly wounded and bleeding'. A fireman used his axe to put the horses out of their misery.

The sound of the raid caused shoppers in neighbouring Lower Thames Street to seek shelter in an alleyway to the side of The Bell public house, but a bomb brought a neighbouring house and part of the pub crashing down, burying the shoppers under the rubble. Eventually rescuers recovered the bodies of four men and dragged seven injured, including a child, from the wreckage.

A few of the raiding aircraft extended across the Thames on their eastward flight dropping bombs close to London Bridge station. The final bombs fell at about 10.40am in Whitechapel, Wapping and the Isle of Dogs as Kleine led Kagohl 3 away from London.

The RFC now had 79 aircraft in the air of 20 different types, while the RNAS put up 22 aircraft. As the incoming formation had headed for London, Higgins redirected individual flights to a position off the north Kent coast where he hoped they would intercept the raiders on their return journey. A series of confused individual attacks harried the Gothas who began to draw their formation together. Many reported problems with jammed guns or an inability to keep up with the raiders. One who did get into close combat, Captain J. Palethorpe, piloting a DH4 from a Testing Squadron, with Air Mechanic F. James as observer, engaged a leading Gotha as it headed across Essex towards

LEFT
Large crowds gather after a bomb hits the roof of the Central Telegraph Office on the morning of 7 July. The bomb damaged the top two floors, injured four and falling masonry killed a sentry in the street. (IWM Q 65536)

RIGHT
Aerial view of London during the raid of 7 July. Geographic key: 1: River Thames. 2: St Paul's Cathedral. 3: Smithfield Market. 4: Finsbury Circus. 5: Liverpool Street Station. Bomb key: A: Central Telegraph Office. B: Aldersgate Street. C: Little Britain. D: Bartholomew Close. E: Golden Lane. F: Whitecross Street. G: Chiswell Street. (IWM Q 108954)

the coast. Palethorpe's Vickers gun jammed but he kept up with the formation allowing James to engage three enemy aircraft with his Lewis gun. James fired off seven drums of ammunition in all and closing in to within 30 or 40 yards (27–37m) of one, he fired into it until it began to emit smoke. But before they could see the outcome a bullet struck Palethorpe 'in the flesh of the hip' and, with blood running down to his boots, he turned sharply away and landed safely at Rochford.

Another crew, flying a No. 50 Squadron Armstrong Whitworth FK8, one of those waiting to intercept the returning Gothas, closed to engage over the North Sea. Flying at 14,000ft (4,270m), the pilot, 2nd Lieutenant F. A. D. Grace with observer, 2nd Lieutenant G. Murray, attacked one Gotha without effect, then attacked a group of three, but turned away because of the intensity of the return fire. Spotting a straggler flying below his FK8, Grace then pounced on this new target, as he later recalled: 'We dived at it, firing our front gun, range 800 yards, as we got closer on a zig-zag course, and when between 600 and 400 yards, we got on its starboard side and above. The observer opened fire on it, with good results, as we saw black smoke coming from the centre section, and the H.A. [hostile aircraft] dived into the sea.'

The Gotha remained on the surface for a while, and although Grace and Murray circled, attempting to alert surface craft, with fuel running low, reluctantly they turned away. Neither the crew nor aircraft were recovered.

Kleine led his formation on a wider return flight in an attempt to avoid the Dunkirk squadrons and in this he was successful, but RNAS pilots from Manston pursued his formation most of the way back to Belgium. Damage from incessant attacks forced one Gotha down on the beach at Ostend and Kagohl 3 lost three others, wrecked on their airfields, a combination of many factors, including enemy action, strong winds, lack of fuel and the Gotha's inherent instability when unladen. British aircrew suffered too with two aircraft shot down.

Back in London there was concern over the number of anti-aircraft shells that had landed on the city adding to the casualties; the London Fire Brigade recorded the fall of 103 shells. Total casualties in the capital reached 54 killed and 190 injured. Of these ten were killed and 55 injured by this 'friendly fire'.

The raid brought a wide variety of reactions. Sections of the bombed population turned against immigrants in their midst, considering many with foreign names to be 'Germans'. Riots broke out in Hackney and Tottenham where mobs wrecked immigrant houses and shops. Moreover, such was the anti-German feeling that four days later King George V (of the Royal House of Saxe-Coburg-Gotha) issued a proclamation announcing that the Royal family name had changed to Windsor.

Feelings of anger were rife against the Government too. The War Cabinet held a series of meetings between 7 and 11 July. Frustrations at the removal of the two 'loaned' squadrons just hours before the raid were voiced and in response a squadron currently forming for service in France was instead earmarked for home service. Another squadron, No. 46, which was operating on the Western Front received orders temporarily redeploying it to England for Home Defence (10 July–30 August). Discussions followed highlighting the limited response to the raid; these resulted in approval for the formation of a committee to consider Home Defence arrangements and the organization of aerial operations.

LONDON MAKES READY

The committee was unusual in that it really revolved around just one man, the former Boer guerrilla leader, now Lieutenant-General Jan Christian Smuts. Having exhaustively interviewed all the senior officers involved, he produced a detailed report on the air defences eight days later. In it he highlighted the flaws in the current system of defence and recommended that a single officer 'of first-rate ability and practical air experience be placed in executive command of the air defence of the London area', bringing together the RFC, AA guns and Observation Corps under a united command. Smuts also called for additional AA guns and the rapid completion and training of three new day-fighter squadrons (Nos. 44, 61 and 112) and a general increase in aircraft committed to the defence of the capital, allowing for the creation of a reserve.

This first part of the report received swift approval leading to the creation of the London Air Defence Area (LADA) on 31 July. The command included all gun batteries in the south-east from Harwich to Dover and inland to London, the nine RFC squadrons allocated to Southern Home Defence wing (Nos. 37, 39, 44, 50, 51, 61, 75, 78 and 112) and all observation posts east of a line drawn between Grantham in Lincolnshire and Portsmouth on the Hampshire coast. The man chosen for the job was Major-General Edward B. Ashmore, a former senior RFC officer and currently commander of the artillery of 29th Division.

The raid of 7 July also raised the question of a public air raid warning again. This time the government felt unable to block the demand and a system of marine distress maroons and police alerts would in future announce incoming raids.

AN ENGLISH SUMMER

While this reorganization was under way London was free from attack. The *Englandgeschwader* waited for its next opportunity but the weather reports were not favourable for attacks on the city. However, clear skies over the coast prompted attacks on Harwich and Felixstowe on 22 July, which resulted in 13 deaths and 26 injuries.

As July passed into August the weather effectively blocked Kleine's ambition and granted Ashmore much-needed time to improve London's defences. The first three weeks of the month heralded a typical English summer – rain and high winds! It proved a disastrous month for Kleine. On 12 August, at short notice, he ordered an attack on Chatham. Strong winds delayed the formation forcing it to attack Southend and Margate instead. Engaged by AA guns and pursued by the RFC and RNAS back across the North Sea, heavy casualties followed: one Gotha shot down at sea, one forced down and crashed near Zeebrugge with four more wrecked in landing accidents.

Kleine ordered two more raids in August on south-eastern coastal towns. Both ended in disaster. On 18 August strong winds forced the formation of 28 Gothas way off course and, with fuel running low, the raid was abandoned. Driven by the wind towards neutral Holland, it appears that Kleine lost as many as nine aircraft to a combination of Dutch AA fire, shortage of fuel and crash landings. Certainly, when the determined Kleine ordered the squadron airborne again four days later, he could muster only 15 aircraft. This raid, on 22 August, proved the futility of the continuance of the daylight campaign. Alerted early to the approach of Kagohl 3, the coastal AA guns were ready and RNAS aircraft in Kent were in the air and waiting. Five Gothas, including Kleine's turned back early with engine problems, the rest ran into a determined defence and turned for home after bombing Margate, Ramsgate and Dover. Three Gothas were shot down, two probably by RNAS aircraft and one by AA fire. While the weather conditions had protected the principal target, London, Kleine lost 18 of Kagohl 3s aircraft in these August daytime raids.

Following the raid of 7 July the Government agreed to a system of air raid warnings. On 14 July an announcement confirmed that in future marine distress maroons fired from fire stations would alert the public of approaching enemy aircraft.

THE 'DAYLIGHT' DEFENCES TIGHTEN

The dogged Lt. Col. Simon submitted a new request for more guns in July, backed by the RFC. He asked for the construction of a new ring of gun stations 25 miles (40km) out from the centre of London, able to put up a barrage of shells to break up the attacking formations before they reached the capital, making them less formidable targets for the RFC to pick off. The scheme required 110 guns covering the north, east and south approaches to the city, but again the request failed. With no new guns available Simon implemented his plan as best he could with ten guns transferred to the eastern approaches from other London stations and a further 24 withdrawn from other duties and redeployed for the defence of London.

In an effort to stem the incidents of AA guns firing at Home Defence squadrons, Ashmore announced the creation of the 'Green Line', a fixed line drawn inside the line of the new outer barrage. Outside the Green Line guns had priority; inside the line priority switched to the defending aircraft. And while the RFC practised the intricacies of flying in formation, elsewhere four BE12 aircraft became the first to be fitted with wireless-telegraphy equipment, enabling them to transmit, but not receive, Morse messages to ground stations

LEFT
While the maroon system was being organized, as a temporary measure, policemen on foot, bicycles and in cars would tour the streets carrying placards emblazoned with 'take cover', accompanied by whistles, bells or motor horns. (C. Ablett)

RIGHT
Further thought on the matter of air raid warnings restricted the use of maroons to day raids only, while the police system continued to warn the population at night – both systems incorporating the use of Boy Scouts blowing bugles to assist in spreading the 'all clear'.

BELOW
Evidence of Kagohl 3's disastrous raid on 22 August 1917. The smouldering wreckage of a Gotha crewed by Oberleutnant Echart Fulda, Unteroffizier Heinrich Schildt and Vizefeldwebel Eichelkamp lying on Hengrove golf course, Margate. All three died. (C. Ablett)

detailing the movements of enemy formations. Moves also commenced to improve telephone communications between Horse Guards and observer posts, airfields and AA gun positions. In addition, a new operations room was under development at Spring Gardens, by Admiralty Arch, Westminster.

August also witnessed a significant development in the history of British aviation. During this month Smuts released the second part of his report, *Air Organization and the Direction of Aerial Operations*. It considered the future of air power and with great insight stated, 'As far as can at present be foreseen, there is absolutely no limit to the scale of [the air service's] future independent war use. And the day may not be far off when aerial operations with their devastation of enemy lands and destruction of industrial and populous centers on a vast scale may become the principal operations of war.'

The report concluded by making a strong recommendation for combining the RFC and RNAS into a single air service and urging its swift implementation. It marked the birth of the Royal Air Force which finally came into being on 1 April 1918.

THE SWITCH TO NIGHT BOMBING

However, all these plans, designed to counter daylight raids, were about to become redundant; the daylight offensive was over. The dramatic losses incurred on recent raids indicated to Kleine the futility of continuing on this course. Therefore, the *Englandgeschwader* prepared for a switch to night flying but retained a hope that the new Gotha variant, the G.V., would revitalize the daylight offensive. These hopes ended when the G.V. failed to offer any significant improvement in performance over the G.IV. After a period of intensive night-flying training, plans were ready in early September 1917 for Kagohl 3 to return to the offensive.

On the night of 3/4 September, before Ashmore's new arrangements were in place, a force of four Gothas attacked Margate, Sheerness and Chatham; it was at the last of these towns that the heaviest casualties occurred when two bombs fell on a drill hall at the naval barracks. When the dust settled 138 naval ratings lay dead amidst the rubble while colleagues dragged the 88 injured clear. The opposition that night proved negligible. With further good weather, the following day Kleine announced a return to London.

At about 8.30pm on 4 September, the first of 11 Gothas took to the air at five-minute intervals. The formations of the daylight campaign were finished, now the aircraft flew singly to avoid collisions in the dark. Inevitably two dropped out with engine problems, leaving the other nine to feel their way with difficulty to England. The first came inland at 10.40pm, the last at 12.10am. Observers struggling to interpret the engine sounds in the dark submitted numerous exaggerated claims about the strength of the incoming Gothas. Eighteen RFC aircraft took off, but only the four Sopwith Camels of No. 44 Squadron and an FK8 of No. 50 Squadron stood any real chance of interception, but no pilots effectively engaged the incoming bombers that night. However, the AA gun at Borstal near Rochester proved more effective. Held for some minutes by a searchlight, the gun targeted a Gotha at a height estimated at 13,000ft (4,000m) and opened fire at 11.27pm. The gun commander, 2nd Lieutenant C. Kendrew, RGA, reported that the Gotha 'was apparently disabled by our gun fire.... A direct hit was then scored and it was observed to fall almost perpendicularly for a short distance turning over and over'. An exhaustive search

discovered no wreckage leading to the presumption that the aircraft came down in the Medway or Thames Estuary and sank. Of the remaining eight Gothas that came inland reports show that just five reached London.

The moon was two days beyond full so the sky was bright over the capital when the first Gotha arrived, although a thin haze hindered the work of the searchlight crews. The lead aircraft dropped its bombs over West Ham and Stratford at around 11.25pm. One fell on an unoccupied factory that had until recently been used as an internment camp for German nationals. Another bombed between Greenwich Park and Woolwich at about 11.45pm.

When the first AA guns in London opened fire '… many people rushed for shelter. Those nearer the tubes went to the stations in all stages of undress and were conveyed in the lifts to the underground platforms. There were hundreds of women and children and scores of men who made for these places of refuge.'

THE FIRST NIGHT-TIME RAID, TUESDAY 4 SEPTEMBER 1917 (pp. 39–39)

On the night of 4 September 1917 a new phenomenon struck London – the first night-time Gotha raid. For almost nine weeks the skies over the city had been free of German aircraft, but now they were back.

That evening 11 Gothas of Kagohl 3 had set out although only five reached the capital. The third of these dropped its first bomb over Oxford Circus shortly before midnight and flew on a south-easterly course towards the Thames. The next three bombs all fell close to the Strand.

Just before these bombs landed, a single-decker 'G' Class London County Council tram, No. 596 **(1)**, had just crossed the Thames on Westminster Bridge and made a stop before continuing along the Victoria Embankment heading towards the Kingsway tunnel. The driver, Alfred Buckle, who, according to his conductor, 69-year-old Joseph Carr, had a premonition that night, was keen to get his shift over. He remarked to Carr before they commenced their final run, 'Joe, mate, I'd give anything not to have to do this last journey'. At Westminster No. 596 halted behind a larger double-decker tram and Buckle

called to its driver, 'Hi, mate, I'm two minutes late. Will you let me pull off in front of you?' A passenger on the double-decker, A. E. Green, recalled. 'Our driver consented, and we waited whilst the single-decker shunted on to our lines. Then we followed closely along behind it'. As Buckle proceeded along Victoria Embankment, the sound of the exploding bombs near the Strand reached him and he accelerated, but just as he passed Cleopatra's Needle **(2)** a 50kg bomb exploded on the pavement between the tram and the ancient monument. The blast smashed through the pavement **(3)**, destroying a gas main, damaging the base of the Needle and an adjacent sphinx **(4)**. The tram took the full blast too. It seared through it, killing Buckle, the two passengers – a man and a woman – and blew Joseph Carr **(5)**, from one end of the tram to the other, but he staggered out onto the street and survived. Eight passers-by were also injured by the blast. Mr Green, in the following tram, recalled that Buckle **(6)** 'appeared to kneel down suddenly, still pulling at his controls. I saw him fall, and that his legs had been blown off: so while dying his last thoughts were to stop his tram.'

A third Gotha appeared at 11.52pm over Oxford Circus in central London and dropped a 50kg bomb, causing serious damage to Bourne and Hollingsworth's store on East Castle Street. Its next bomb fell in Agar Street, off the Strand, outside the main entrance to the Charing Cross Hospital. A man, H. Stockman, was about to take shelter in a hotel entrance opposite where two others already stood. But at that moment, 'a woman came up with terror written on her face'. Mr Stockman, realizing there was room only for three, indicated to the woman to take the place, for which she thanked him profusely. Moments later the bomb exploded and blew the gallant Stockman to the ground. When he looked up he realized the women was dead. An RFC officer on leave, standing on the corner of Agar Street, rushed to help and, seeing the demolished front of the hotel, stepped into the building. There he found '… two Colonial [Canadian] soldiers sitting dead in their chairs. One had been killed by a piece of the bomb, which went through the back of his head and out of the front of his Army hat, taking the cap badge with it.'

Besides these three deaths, another ten lay injured, including three soldiers, an American naval rating and a policeman. Across the Strand a bomb damaged the roof of the Little Theatre, converted into a soldier's canteen by the Canadian YMCA, and another fell in Victoria Embankment Gardens, just missing the Hotel Cecil. Then, seconds later, a fourth 50kg bomb of this salvo exploded on the Victoria Embankment, close to Cleopatra's Needle, just as a single-decker tram passed. The blast seared through the tram killing the driver and two passengers but the bewildered conductor, Joseph Carr, staggered clear. (See the colour plate on pp. 38/39).

A few bombs dropped on Wanstead at around 11.55pm, then, about 30 minutes later, the fifth Gotha appeared. At about 12.30am bombs dropped on Edmonton, followed by explosions in Tottenham, Hornsey, Crouch End and Upper Holloway, where a bomb demolished the laundry of the Islington Workhouse in St John's Road. Another fell harmlessly in Highgate, just east of Hampstead Heath, followed by two bombs, both of 12kg, which landed in Kentish Town. One of these, falling in Wellesley Road, damaged the doors and

LEFT
A bronze sphinx guarding Cleopatra's Needle on the Victoria Embankment. At about midnight on 4 September a 50kg bomb exploded close to the ancient monument, the blast hitting a passing tram, killing the driver and two passengers.

RIGHT
The demolished laundry of the Islington Workhouse in St John's Road (now St John's Way) in Upper Holloway. A 50kg bomb landed at around 12.30am on 5 September but there were no casualties.

A diagram illustrating the new barrage fire system, producing curtains of concentrated fire in the path of incoming aircraft. Barrages were fixed on map coordinates and bore code-names such as Jig-saw, Bubbly, Knave of Hearts and Cosy Corner.

windows of 15 houses but also claimed lives too. A witness reported seeing '… a flash in the air, and immediately afterwards there was a tremendous explosion. A dense volume of smoke was rising from the road'.

As the smoke cleared the bodies of a soldier, home on hospital leave, and a woman with her five-year-old child were revealed, dead in the passageway of the house where they lived. The soldier had just pushed his mother clear, saving her life, when the bomb exploded. Further bombs landed in Primrose Hill and Regent's Park before the two final bombs fell close to Edgware Road at about 12.50am. One of these, in Norfolk Crescent, killed a woman, while the other exploded in the air above Titchborne Street (no longer there, it was just south of the present Sussex Gardens). The blast caught an 11-year-old girl as she walked to the end of the road to see if the 'all-clear' had sounded and bowled her along the street. Having convinced herself she was still alive, she made her way home. Only then did she realize, 'I had a hole through my knee. Also, the frock I was wearing had 15 holes in it where I had been whirled along and struck by shrapnel.' The bomb injured 16 people caught in the blast, one of whom later died, damaged 33 houses in Titchborne Street, and blew out the windows of 12 shops in Edgware Road. That sound of smashing glass signalled the end of the raid and silence gradually returned to the skies over London.

DEFENSIVE IMPROVEMENTS

The switch to night-bombing presented Britain's defences with a new threat. The War Cabinet called again on the indefatigable Smuts and on 6 September he produced another report. Smuts doubted the ability of aircraft to engage enemy raiders at night, but recommended the use of more powerful searchlights, hoping to dazzle the incoming pilots. He also supported the idea just proposed by Ashmore for a balloon barrage, 'a wire screen suspended from balloons and intended to form a sort of barrage in which the enemy machine navigated at night will be caught'. Experiments began and approval was given for 20 of these screens, although ultimately only ten were raised, the first in October 1917.

After the first moonlit raid, the weather turned in favour of the defenders, granting them time to hone the defensive arrangements to meet this new threat. Investigations into new methods of sound-location continued and Ashmore's plan for the Green Line became operational. No British aircraft were to fly beyond the outer gun line or over London. The AA guns were now authorized to consider any aircraft in these areas as hostile. Within these cleared areas

The 4/5 September 1917 raid

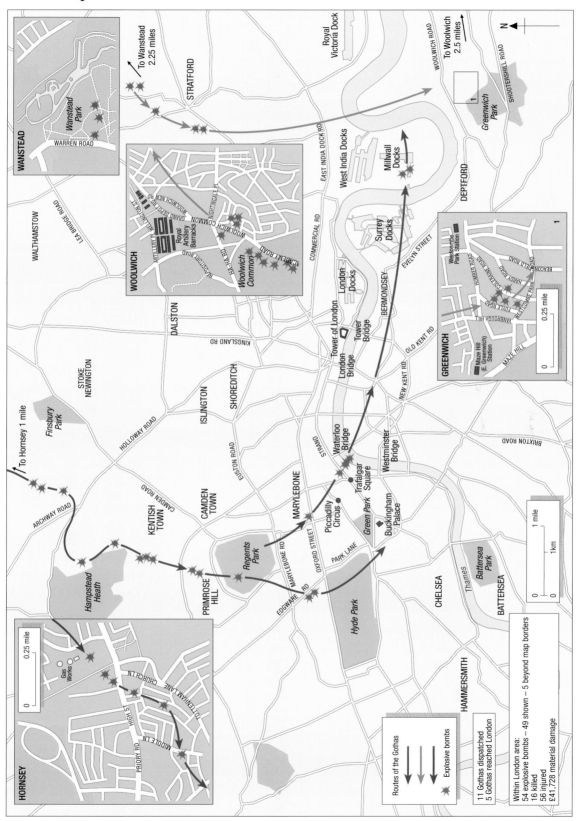

N

WANSTEAD

To Wanstead 2.25 miles

Wanstead Park

WARREN ROAD

STRATFORD

Royal Victoria Dock

WOOLWICH ROAD

To Woolwich 2.5 miles

SHOOTERSHILL ROAD

1

Greenwich Park

LEA BRIDGE ROAD

WALTHAMSTOW

WOOLWICH

ARTILLERY PL
RESTTON ROAD
HA-HA RD
GRAND DEPOT ROAD
WOOLWICH NEW RD
NIGHTINGALE PL
ACADEMY ROAD

Royal Artillery Barracks

Woolwich Common

EAST INDIA DOCK RD

West India Docks

Millwall Docks

DEPTFORD

GREENWICH

1

Westcombe Park Station

BEACONSFIELD ROAD
WESTCOMBE PARK ROAD
HARDY ROAD
HUMBER ROAD
COLERAINE ROAD
FOYLE ROAD

Westcombe Park

Maze Hill
(E. Greenwich) Station

VANBRUGH HILL

MAZE HILL

0   0.25 mile

STOKE NEWINGTON

Finsbury Park

To Hornsey 1 mile

HOLLOWAY ROAD

KINGSLAND RD

DALSTON

ISLINGTON

SHOREDITCH

EUSTON ROAD

COMMERCIAL RD

London Docks

Tower of London

Tower Bridge

London Bridge

Surrey Docks

BERMONDSEY

EVELYN STREET

OLD KENT RD

NEW KENT RD

BRIXTON ROAD

ARCHWAY ROAD

CAMDEN ROAD

KENTISH TOWN

CAMDEN TOWN

Regents Park

MARYLEBONE RD

MARYLEBONE

Waterloo Bridge

STRAND

Trafalgar Square

Westminster Bridge

Hampstead Heath

PRIMROSE HILL

Primrose Hill

EDGWARE RD

OXFORD STREET

Piccadilly Circus

Green Park

PARK LANE

Buckingham Palace

Hyde Park

CHELSEA

Battersea Park

Thames

BATTERSEA

HAMMERSMITH

HORNSEY

Gas Works

HIGH ST
PRIORY RD
TOTTENHAM LANE
CHURCH LN
MIDDLE LN

0   0.25 mile

0   1 mile
0   1km

0   1km

Routes of the Gothas

Explosive bombs

11 Gothas dispatched
5 Gothas reached London

Within London area:
54 explosive bombs – 49 shown – 5 beyond map borders
16 killed
56 injured
£41,728 material damage

43

'Giant' *R.33*, an R.VI type, designed by the Zeppelin works at Staaken. These huge four-engine aircraft, significantly larger than any Luftwaffe aircraft that attacked London in World War II, had a wingspan of 138ft (42m), almost twice the size of the Gothas.

Simon developed a new system of barrage fire which directed guns to direct 'curtains' of shellfire in specific locations, with these walls of fire extending over 2,500ft (760m) from top to bottom, targeted at varying heights between 5,000 and 17,000ft (1,500 and 5,000m). With each barrage screen fixed by map reference, a coordinator directed different barrages to commence firing as an enemy aircraft progressed across the plotting table. Once held by searchlights the AA guns could switch from barrage fire to direct fire against the enemy bomber.

While grounded by the weather, Kleine received the news that a new squadron was about to join the attacks on London. In September 1917 the OHL transferred Riesenflugzeug Abteilung (Rfa) 501 from the Eastern Front, via Berlin, to Belgium. Riesenflugzeug Abteilung 501 had been flying early versions of the R-type – *Riesenflugzeug* (Giant aircraft) – since August 1916. Now the commander of Rfa 501, Hauptmann Richard von Bentivegni, received R-types of the latest design, the R.VI, designed by the Zeppelin works at Staaken (as well as the single model R.IV and R.V types). Somewhat ungainly in appearance, the Staaken R.VI, with its crew of seven, was advanced for its time, boasting an enclosed cockpit for the two pilots, navigational aids including wireless telegraphy (W/T) equipment, and could carry a large bomb load, including bombs of 100, 300 and even 1,000kg. On 22 September the first aircraft of Rfa 501 arrived at Sint-Denijs-Westrem, sharing the airfield with two flights of Kagohl 3, and began to prepare their aircraft for their first raid on London. They were not yet operational when favourable weather was forecast for Monday 24 September, the start of an intense period of bombing – later known as the Harvest Moon Offensive – during which six raids took place over a period of eight days.

THE HARVEST MOON OFFENSIVE

Sixteen Gothas set out on the raid but three turned back with technical problems. The remaining 13 crossed the English coastline between Orfordness and Dover. The wide-ranging courses of these attacks meant the 30 RFC aircraft that took off to intercept the raid – including the first use of Biggin Hill airfield by the RFC – saw nothing, and similarly the searchlights struggled to pick out the raiders. However, only three bombers penetrated inland to London, six contented themselves with a bombardment of Dover while the remaining four dropped their bombs on coastal targets in south Essex and north Kent. Those that did battle through to London found the new AA barrage fire system in

LEFT
The bomb that fell on 144a King's Cross Road killed 13-year-old James Sharpe and injured seven others. Having helped his mother carry his brothers and sisters across the road to a shelter, James returned to help his invalid grandfather just as the bomb exploded, burying him under the rubble of the building. He died from a fractured skull. (IWM HO 72)

RIGHT
The blasted façade of the Bedford Hotel in Southampton Row. A 50kg bomb landed in the road outside the hotel at about 8.55pm on 24 September killing 13 and injuring 22. All the windows in the hotel are smashed.

operation. The first to approach did so over the eastern suburbs and dropped its first bomb, an incendiary, on Lodore Street, just off East India Dock Road, around 8.05pm, followed quickly by a couple more on Poplar, just north of the West India Docks. Then it crossed the Thames and dropped four bombs on Rotherhithe and Deptford before turning away and heading east. The effectiveness of the new barrage impressed those watching on the ground: 'Everyone agreed that the intensity of the bombardment from the anti-aircraft guns was the greatest yet experienced.… A searchlight succeeded in finding one of the raiders.… Shrapnel was bursting all around, and more than once it looked as if the aeroplane would be brought crashing to earth… after a shell had burst in front of him he banked steeply and made off in the opposite direction, followed by a violent bombardment, until he disappeared from view.'

The other two Gothas came in over north London around 8.35pm, dropping a mixture of explosive and incendiary bombs on Islington before heading towards the centre of the city. An explosive bomb that fell in King's Cross Road caused much local damage and killed 13-year-old James Sharpe.

Elsewhere a bomb exploded outside the Bedford Hotel on Southampton Row, Bloomsbury. A doctor, R. D. MacGregor, on his way to have dinner at the hotel heard the bomb falling and, diving through the door, shouted a warning to a small group gathered there. Doctor MacGregor survived but the bomb killed 13, including three hotel staff, and injured 22. Damage nearby was extensive.

The bomb made a hole in the roadway some 4ft (1m) deep, the force of the explosion blowing out all the windows in front of the building, even to the sixth storey, and shattering the glass in most of the houses on either side of the street for several hundred yards.

Moments later another 50kg bomb crashed through the glass roof of the Royal Academy in Piccadilly, causing considerable damage to the building and, even before the dust had settled, the next bomb fell at the north-east corner of Green Park.

The tally for the night was 13 explosive bombs and 19 incendiaries with a total of 14 killed and 49 injured. Reports showed that one Gotha crashed on landing in Belgium, possibly having suffered damage from AA guns on the homeward journey. However, the increased anti-aircraft barrage fire resulted in

Just seconds after the bomb on the Royal Academy another gouged a crater in Green Park. The blast smashed the windows of the Ritz and numerous other exclusive homes nearby.

the police recording damage caused by 73 AA shells: one, landing in Cloudesley Road, Islington, injured five. Another dramatic change that night was the number of people who rushed to the nearest Underground station when the police gave the 'take cover' warning shortly before 8.00pm. The Government estimated 100,000 Londoners went underground that night; the trend was to continue and grow.

When the warning sounded again the following night the crowding in the Underground was beginning to be a problem, with the authorities growing concerned by the exodus from the East End. *The Times* blamed it on the 'alien population of the East-end' who they claimed, arrived in family groups to camp out on the platforms 'as early as 5 o'clock in the afternoon'.

The Gothas returned the following night, Tuesday 25 September. Fifteen Gothas set out to attack London, but this time only one dropped out with technical problems. Crossing the coast between Foulness and Dover from about 7.00 to 7.45pm, most settled on targets on the north-east Kent coast, such as Margate and Folkestone, with only three penetrating to the south-eastern corner of London. One of these arrived later than the first two, dropping three bombs over Blackheath, all of which failed to explode, and one on Charlton Park before turning away in the face of the barrage. Twenty defence aircraft took off, but again all but one failed to locate the incoming aircraft. Unfortunately for those living in the area where the other two aircraft dropped their bombs, it appears no 'take cover' warning reached them and many were out in the streets when the bombs began to fall. One of the first landed in Marcia Road, just off the Old Kent Road, shortly before 8.00pm. The bomb landed in the street, smashing a gas main and wrecking about 20 houses and 'in the whole length of it there was not a pane of glass left intact'.

A woman living on the top floor of one of the houses had rushed upstairs to turn off the gas when she saw through a window 'a great ball of flame falling towards us'. She remembered no more until, having crashed down to the ground floor, she heard her sister calling as helping hands dragged her carefully from the

The 24 September 1917 raid

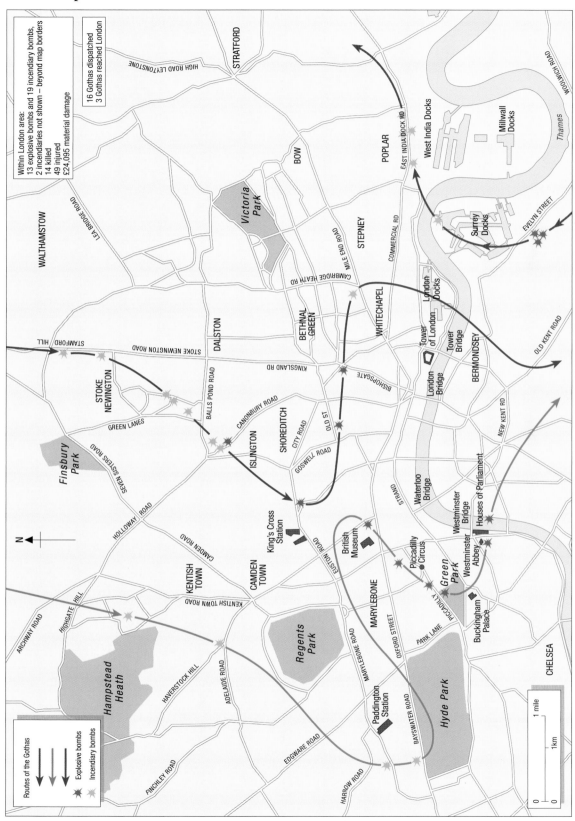

Within London area:
13 explosive bombs and 19 incendiary bombs,
2 incendiaries not shown – beyond map borders
14 killed
49 injured
£24,095 material damage

16 Gothas dispatched
3 Gothas reached London

Routes of the Gothas

Explosive bombs
Incendiary bombs

rubble. She survived with injuries just to her legs. Others in the street were not so lucky; three died and another 16 were injured, one of whom later died.

Just a few yards away in Old Kent Road another bomb fell directly on Tew's Bakery. The owner of the business had constructed a bunker of heavy flour sacks in the bakehouse under his shop. The family were just sitting down to supper when, as one of the baker's daughters explained, a cry went up in the street. '"They're here!" We all made a rush to our bakehouse, as did many neighbours. The moment we were there there was a terrifying crash, and we knew the house had been struck. The dreadful noise and the sudden darkness; the choking dust; the screaming; the continuous tumbling of the ruin above us, we shall always remember.'

It was a terrible experience, but all 17 people huddled in the bake-house survived uninjured to tell their story.

The Gotha dropped further 50kg bombs close by in Mina Road, Odell Street, Coburg Road and Goldie Street. The accompanying aircraft dropped a string of 16 incendiary bombs in New Cross and Deptford, with one landing uncomfortably close to the South Metropolitan Gas Company off Old Kent Road.

At about 8.15pm a Sopwith 1½ Strutter of No. 78 squadron with Captain D. J. Bell and 2nd Lieutenant G. G. Williams on board was flying south of Brentwood when it came under attack. The enemy aircraft was flying east, presumably returning from London. The Sopwith took up the chase and for 15 minutes kept it in sight, firing frequent bursts before the target disappeared from view. The following day the press carried a story about a substantial amount of petrol falling in Essex, suggesting damage to one of the Gotha's fuel tanks. Certainly one Gotha failed to return, lost over the sea, possibly having run out of fuel.

The weather then turned against Kagohl 3 once more, with the return of rain and heavy cloud. But in London the nightly exodus to the Underground continued. In fact the skies over the Belgian airfields did not begin to clear until the afternoon of Friday 28 September. Kleine gathered 25 Gothas for the raid

A Gotha G.V being loaded with two 100kg and five 50kg bombs, a total weight of 450kg – just under half a ton – a fairly typical weight for a night raid. (IWM Q 108844)

and this time Bentivegni had two of his R-type 'Giants' ready too. It was the largest force yet assembled against London. However, serious doubts surfaced about the weather just before take-off, forcing Kleine and Bentivegni to issue orders to their crews to turn back if they encountered solid cloud cover. Fifteen did just that and only three Gothas and the two 'Giants' claimed to have dropped any bombs, but none got close to London. The cloud cover meant few anti-aircraft guns opened fire and those that did were just firing in the general direction of the engine noise. Oberleutnant Fritz Lorenz, commanding Kasta 14 of the *Englandgeschwader*, left a rather poetic description of his flight over England on this occasion: 'Probing in vain, the searchlights painted large yellow saucers in the clouds below us. Where a devil's cauldron of bursting shrapnel had never let a machine pass without inflicting at least some hits, there prevailed this time in this silvery solitude a peace which was like something out of a fairy tale.'

But this peaceful interlude soon came to an abrupt end. The journey turned from fairy tale to nightmare for many. Three crews never returned, believed shot down by AA guns at Deal, Ramsgate and Sheppey while five Gothas crashed in Belgium and one in Holland – a third of all attacking aircraft lost.

Yet even though no aircraft reached London there were casualties in the city. Anticipating the incoming raid the 'take cover' warning went out just before 8.00pm. Suddenly there was a rush by about 200 to 300 people for the entrance of the Underground at Liverpool Street Station. Four policemen on duty there tried to stem the tide, but as one reported, 'there was a panic, they lost their heads'. By the time the police had fought their way down the crowded stairs where 'people were packed like sardines', they found a heap of eight bodies. According to a newspaper report the following day: 'Eight cases of injury were reported… chiefly of broken limbs and body injuries. One elderly woman was crushed to death and another, whose breastbone was fractured, is not expected to live. A child reported to be killed was taken away on an ambulance.'

THE ARRIVAL OF THE 'GIANTS'

Although the raid had made a large dent in the strength of Kagohl 3, the relentless Kleine ordered another attack the next evening, Saturday 29 September. He mustered just seven Gothas while Rfa 501 prepared three R.VI 'Giants' for the attack. Over England the force encountered cloud while a low ground mist hampered the Home Defence squadrons. Many observers, searchlight and gun crews were confused by the sheer noise generated by the massive four-engine 'Giants', whose existence was not yet general knowledge, submitting reports mistaking single aircraft as groups of incoming Gothas. The RNAS sent three aircraft up from the airfield at Manston while the RFC put 30 aircraft in the air, but there were only three brief sightings of hostile aircraft.

German sources report that just two Gothas and one of the R.VI 'Giants' – R.39 – reached the capital. The exact courses taken by the raiders over the capital are hard to define but one headed much further west than usual, dropping a bomb on Notting Hill and two on Putney Common (now Barnes Common) in south-west London, possibly attempting to extinguish a searchlight based there. One of these killed a married couple, 47-year-old George Lyell and his wife, who were walking on the common when the bomb landed. The blast left Lyell's body 'about six yards from where the bomb fell, and the woman on the other side of the road'. A string of five 50kg bombs landed in a line from

Waterloo Station to Kennington. The bomb at Waterloo caused extensive damage around the station while another just south of the station, in Mead Row, injured five people and severely damaged 14 houses. A further bomb fell on the lawn of the Bethlem Hospital Lunatic Asylum in Lambeth (now home to the Imperial War Museum); the patients and staff had a miraculous escape as reported in the press: 'Then a remarkable thing happened. One of the patients shouted to the others to lie flat on the ground, and they did so. Immediately there was a loud report and a crashing of glass, woodwork and stone… the bomb had fallen in the grounds of the building, not fifty yards away. Hundreds of windows had been shattered…. Yet there was not a single casualty.'

North of the Thames there were two main concentrations of bombs, one on an east–west line across Haggerston and Dalston where nine 12kg explosive bombs fell, and another running north-west across Islington towards Hampstead Heath.

In Dalston two bombs fell in Shrublands Road. One exploded in a back garden killing two children, William and Ethel Lee, who were in the kitchen with their parents. In another house, at 34 Mortimer Road, two women were sheltering with nine children when a bomb exploded, again in the back garden. The blast smashed through the kitchen window killing a soldier's wife, 32-year-old Mabel Ward, and her six-year-old son Percy.

However, the worst casualty list of the night came in Holloway at The Eaglet public house. On hearing the 'take cover' warning, the landlord, Edward Crouch, sent his wife and child down to the cellar to take cover. A number of customers and passers-by rushed down too but Crouch remained in the bar counting the takings. Moments later a 50kg bomb 'struck the wooden cellar flap just outside the entrance, penetrated to the cellar, and exploded forcing everything upwards'. The stunned landlord's last memory was of a terrific crash and the floor blown to pieces. The intense explosion killed his wife and three others and injured 32.

The intense anti-aircraft barrage probably forced the raiders to turn away early. One newspaper reported that the bombardment was 'unprecedented in this country' and went on to remind its readers that 'Shrapnel cases and bullets, if fired into the air, must obviously fall somewhere, and it is utter folly for people to stand about in the streets, in open doorways, or at windows.'

This was a very real danger. That night the police recorded 276 anti-aircraft shells falling on London; two landing in Chiswick High Road injured 11, one in Goldhawk Road, Shepherd's Bush, killed a man and elsewhere across the city another 13 people were injured. That night estimates show some 300,000 people took shelter in Underground stations.

The 29 September 1917 raid

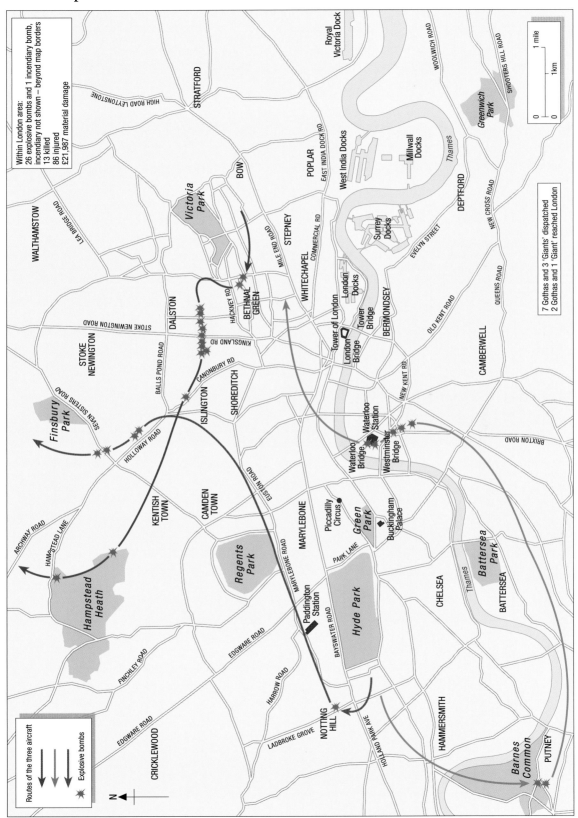

Within London area:
26 explosive bombs and 1 incendiary bomb,
incendiary not shown – beyond map borders
13 killed
86 injured
£21,987 material damage

7 Gothas and 3 'Giants' dispatched
2 Gothas and 1 'Giant' reached London

Routes of the three aircraft

Explosive bombs

N

WALTHAMSTOW

STRATFORD

HIGH ROAD LEYTONSTONE

LEA BRIDGE ROAD

BOW

Victoria Park

STOKE NEWINGTON ROAD

DALSTON

HACKNEY RD

BETHNAL GREEN

MILE END ROAD

STEPNEY

WHITECHAPEL

COMMERCIAL RD

POPLAR

EAST INDIA DOCK RD

Royal Victoria Dock

WOOLWICH ROAD

SHOOTERS HILL ROAD

Greenwich Park

1 mile

1 km

0

0

West India Docks

Millwall Docks

Thames

DEPTFORD

NEW CROSS ROAD

STOKE NEWINGTON

BALLS POND ROAD

KINGSLAND RD

CANONBURY RD

ISLINGTON

SHOREDITCH

Tower of London

London Docks

Tower Bridge

London Bridge

BERMONDSEY

Surrey Docks

EVELYN STREET

OLD KENT RD

QUEENS ROAD

CAMBERWELL

SEVEN SISTERS ROAD

Finsbury Park

HOLLOWAY ROAD

Waterloo Station

Waterloo Bridge

Westminster Bridge

NEW KENT RD

BRIXTON ROAD

ARCHWAY ROAD

HAMPSTEAD LANE

KENTISH TOWN

CAMDEN TOWN

EUSTON ROAD

MARYLEBONE

Piccadilly Circus

Green Park

Buckingham Palace

Hampstead Heath

FINCHLEY ROAD

Regents Park

MARYLEBONE ROAD

Paddington Station

PARK LANE

Hyde Park

CHELSEA

Battersea Park

Thames

BATTERSEA

EDGWARE ROAD

BAYSWATER ROAD

HARROW ROAD

LADBROKE GROVE

NOTTING HILL

HOLLAND PARK AVE

HAMMERSMITH

Barnes Common

PUTNEY

CRICKLEWOOD

EDGWARE ROAD

51

The attacking aircraft did not get away without loss either. One Gotha crashed in Holland, resulting in internment for the crew, and it appears likely that the Dover AA guns shot down another over the sea.

If the hard-pressed defences hoped for a lull in the attacks to enable them to take stock they were to be disappointed; the following night – 30 September – the raiders returned again. It was the night of the full moon, the weather in London had been good and the population waited nervously, expecting another attack. Kleine mustered just 11 Gothas for the attack, and then, as usual, once airborne one quickly dropped out. The attacking aircraft came in between 6.45 and 8.15pm. The RFC flew 35 defensive sorties in response with the RNAS putting up two aircraft from Manston. According to an RFC report, 'Three pilots thought that they saw Hostile machines and two of these pilots opened fire', but without result. Once again the over-worked gun barrage prepared to deflect the attack. Out in the western sub-command of the London guns, Lieutenant-Colonel Alfred Rawlinson bleakly summed up his command: owing to cuts in personnel he had '… the very smallest number of men which would suffice to work the guns… these men were necessarily of indifferent physique, such as did not permit their employment at the Front… they were hurriedly and recently trained… there were no reserves, and it was therefore necessary to keep every man, however exhausted, at his post at all costs…'

On the night of 30 September Rawlinson reported that a number of his guns each fired 'over 500 rounds'. With the barrels becoming red hot, and despite pouring cold water over them, he had to call 'cease fire' at times to assist cooling. The hot barrels also caused rounds to jam. In an attempt to get the guns firing again as soon as possible he issued the extremely dangerous non-regulation order, 'Jam another round in behind it and fire it out'.

According to one newspaper account, 'it was just half past seven when the distant booming of the guns was heard' and the reporter watched and listened as, 'Closer and closer came the noise of guns until it developed into a veritable roar.' The barrage fire was intense and threatening to the attacking crews. Reports indicate that only six aircraft reached London that night but their stay over the capital was brief and generally ineffective; the police and fire service recorded only 22 explosive and 14 incendiary bombs. Most of the damage occurred in East London where bombs fell in Wanstead, Poplar, Plaistow and Barking. At Fairfoot Road, Bromley-by-Bow, 'a narrow thoroughfare of two-storeyed residences', a bomb fell on No. 3, completely demolishing it, killing an 80-year-old man, and injuring a sailor on leave, his wife, another woman and a child. It also damaged another 12 houses in the road. About

three-quarters of a mile to the south, a bomb on Southill Street, Poplar, injured nine and two bombs exploded around the Midland Railway cleaning sheds at Durban Road, West Ham, damaging three locomotives. In north London a string of bombs fell across Archway and Highgate with the last three falling in Parliament Fields where they damaged a cricket pavilion. Finally, in south-east London two explosive and two incendiary bombs fell in and around the Woolwich Royal Dockyard, with most damage occurring around Trinity Road.

In spite of the intensity of the aerial barrage – just over 14,000 shells fired over London and south-east England (9,000 by LADA) at the ten raiding aircraft – and the claims of a Dover gun crew to have brought down a homeward-bound Gotha, all aircraft appear to have returned safely. Total casualties of the raid were one killed and 19 injured by bombs with another two killed and 12 injured by AA shells.

Undeterred, Kleine ordered Kagohl 3 to attack again the next night, Monday 1 October. In London that night the weather was fine; there was good visibility with little wind and no clouds, but a ground mist increased during the night hindering German navigation and preventing some British squadrons getting airborne. Kleine dispatched 18 Gothas but it appears six turned back. The leading aircraft crossed the coast at 6.50pm, the last not until two hours later. The RFC managed to get 18 aircraft in the air but only one pilot caught a brief glimpse of a raider. The AA guns experienced problems too. The constant firing over the last few days meant many were running short of ammunition and others – with a lifespan estimated at 1,500 rounds – were coming to the end of their usefulness. To preserve them as long as possible an order restricted each burst of barrage fire that night to last no longer than one minute.

A combination of the barrage fire and ground mist meant that perhaps only six Gothas arrived over London, dropping bombs between 8.00 and 10.00pm. The first bomb fell in north London near the Edmonton Gas Works, followed by one that fell directly in the Serpentine in Hyde Park, then four 50kg bombs landed in Belgravia and Pimlico close to Victoria Station. One of these bombs, dropping in Glamorgan Street, claimed the lives of four friends sheltering from the raid. Frederick Hanton and Leo Fitzgerald, both 18, and George Fennimore

LEFT
A cutaway diagram showing a Gotha commander using his Goertz bombsight.

RIGHT
Caesar Street (now Nazrul Street), near Kingsland Road, suffered badly on the night of 1 October. Three 50kg bombs fell on the street, demolishing numbers 21, 23 and 41, causing major damage to 11 houses and lesser damage to 40 others.

and Henry Greenway, both 17, all played for the same football team and all died in the blast, killed by splinters from the bomb. A few bombs landed in the Highbury–Finsbury Park area; one in Canning Road, Highbury, killed Harriet Sears, a 78-year-old woman, and damaged 36 houses. The most damage though was concentrated within a few streets in Shoreditch, between Haggerston and Hoxton. In a matter of seconds 16 50kg bombs fell on a north–south line parallel with the Kingsland Road. The police records show that these bombs damaged about 770 houses (damage ranging from houses demolished to windows smashed); they also killed four people living in Hows Street and injured eight in Maria Street, six in Caesar Street, two in both Laburnum Street and Pearson Street, and one in Nichol Square.

Shortly after 10.00pm the last raider departed the skies over London and 'the firing practically ceased, only an occasional distant boom of the guns being heard, and all was quiet at 10.20.' It was of course anything but a quiet night for those left searching for casualties amongst the piles of rubble that had moments before been homes. Total losses in London that night amounted to 11 killed and 41 injured, with material damage in and around the capital estimated at £44,500.

Although Londoners could not know it at the time, the raid of 1 October 1917 marked the end of the Harvest Moon offensive. A dramatic change in the weather put a halt to further raids by Kagohl 3 for the next four weeks. Five raids had reached London in the eight days of the offensive, yet from a German viewpoint the results were disappointing; the authorities recorded 151 bombs in London (94 explosive and 57 incendiary) with material damage estimated at £117,773 and casualties confirmed at 50 killed and 229 injured. However, the raids were producing some of the effects outlined in the orders for Operation *Türkenkreuz*; production of munitions at Woolwich Arsenal fell significantly during the raids. And many Londoners, a great number of whom now regularly slept on crowded and insanitary station platforms, were suffering from stress and shattered nerves.

A BRIEF RESPITE

In this welcome lull, efforts to improve the ammunition supply to the AA guns were successful and the poor condition of the guns received attention; each month 20 worn-out guns were scheduled for relining. In addition, the production output of 3in. 20cwt AA guns for October, earmarked for arming merchant ships, was reassigned to the London defences, while local authorities began requisitioning buildings with suitable basements as shelters and the press were told to moderate their reports of the bombing. The first two of the proposed balloon aprons, approved to cover the approaches to London, from Tottenham in the north around the east via Wanstead, Ilford, Barking, Plumstead to Lewisham, south-east of the city, were in operation in early October. Both were in Essex, one about a mile (2km) south-east of Barking and the other about 2 miles (3km) east of Ilford. To aid sound detection, experiments were under way with a 'sound reflector' cut into the chalk cliffs near Dover – first used during the night of the 1 October raid. Other experiments using pairs of horns fixed on vertical and horizontal arms – sound locators – proved that when accurately adjusted they could give a trained operator an indication of the height, direction and distance of incoming aircraft. And after much public pressure the government authorized a committee to

investigate retaliatory bombing of German towns and cities. The RFC and RNAS were already bombing the Kagohl 3 airfields in Belgium and at the end of September these nagging attacks on Sint-Denijs-Westrem and Melle-Gontrode forced Kleine to redistribute the *Kasta* around the Ghent airfields. On 4 October, in a brief respite from the stresses of command, Kleine received the Pour Le Mérite in recognition of his recent London raids. Meanwhile, while Kleine waited for a forecast of good weather, the pilots of the RFC continued to familiarize themselves with the complexities of flying their latest fighter aircraft at night.

THE BOMBERS RETURN

With an improvement in the weather, Kleine prepared the *Englandgeschwader* for an attack on the night of 31 October, the day after the full moon. He mustered 22 Gothas, and this time they all reached England. Kleine hoped the staggered take-off pattern would ensure a constant flow of raiders over London for a three-hour period, and with half the bombs loaded this time being incendiaries he hoped to start major fires all over the city. The first aircraft crossed the Kent coast at about 10.45pm, the rest came inland, singly or in pairs, over the next two and a half hours. Many, however, were pushed north by crosswinds, abandoned London as a target and attacked towns in Kent instead. German reports claim ten continued to the capital but there were only three main areas that were bombed, suggesting that three aircraft reached south London with perhaps another two getting as far as Erith on the south-eastern approaches. Certainly some 11 explosive and 20 incendiary bombs fell on Erith and neighbouring Slade Green at around 11.45pm – of these, two of the explosive bombs and six of the incendiaries were duds.

Over London clouds began gathering at about 10,000ft (3,000m), hindering the searchlights and guns – this resulted in the LADA guns firing only 2,000 shells. In the city '... the warning was soon followed by the report

LEFT
Women workers checking small-arms ammunition at Woolwich Arsenal. The Gotha raids seriously disrupted output. On the night of 24 September production of .303in. rifle ammunition dropped by 84 per cent and the following night it was down by 77 per cent. (IWM Q 27853)

RIGHT
Balloon apron cables extended for 1,000 yards (910m), held aloft by three balloons. From the cable 1,000ft-long (300m) steel wires hung down, 25 yards (23m) apart, their purpose being to force attacking aircraft up to a predictable height where the AA guns could concentrate their fire as well as presenting an obstacle to incoming raiders.

of distant gunfire, heavy, rapid and muffled. Presently nearer guns joined in the bombardment, and then for nearly a couple of hours sleep was impossible.'

An attack developed over the Isle of Dogs at about 12.45am, possibly by two aircraft, when a bomb that dropped on Maria Street, just off West Ferry Road, damaged about 100 houses. Further bombs fell on Greenwich Park, where an incendiary just missed the Royal Observatory and three others fell between the entrance to the Blackwall Tunnel and South Metropolitan Gas Works, but two of them, both incendiaries, failed to ignite. Another incendiary fell on the works of a paint company based on the Thames at Charlton where it burnt out a storeroom, before eight explosive bombs dropped harmlessly over the Belvedere marshes as the aircraft headed home.

The final attack of the night developed over Tooting in south-west London at about 1.30am, marked by a steady string of 13 explosive bombs between there and Streatham. In Crockerton Road a bomb killed two people standing in an open doorway and injured two others. Half a mile further on, in Romberg Road, three died, one of them, 13-year-old Boy Scout Alfred Page, while waiting to go out and sound the 'all clear' on his bugle. The bomb also killed his father and injured a woman and two children. An eyewitness recalled that 'the roof of the house, the walls, and the furniture were reduced to a chaotic mass of brick and plaster, wood and iron'. From Streatham the aircraft appears to have headed out in north-easterly direction, dropping bombs on Deptford, Surrey Docks, Millwall Docks and Plaistow as it went.

For Kleine, however, the results were again disappointing. Although 22 aircraft had reached England only 40 explosive and 37 incendiaries (12 of which failed to ignite) were recorded in London, amounting to damage calculated at just £9,536 of which £2,000 was on outlying Erith. Casualties were minimal too: eight killed and 19 injured (five of these by AA shells). And Kleine's disappointment did not end there. Back in Belgium the returning bomber crews found their arrival coinciding with the appearance of a rolling bank of fog. A returning Gotha circled the airfield and later one of the crew recalled that '... the fog showed no sign of thinning, but staying airborne for

Officers of Kagohl 3 assembled outside Château Drory, the squadron's headquarters at Melle-Gontrode, on the outskirts of Ghent, in 1917. Rudolph Kleine, commander of the Englandgeschwader, is standing on the left of the photograph. (IWM Q 108839)

much longer was impossible; our fuel reserves were almost exhausted.... We sank into the fog, with no feeling for our positioning in the air, dropping into the unknown.... Death lurked below us, ready to pounce. Seconds lasted for eternities, then: There! The ground! We were safe!'

Other crews were not so fortunate; five crashed and wrecked their aircraft attempting landings in the fog. Bad weather meant it would be over a month before Kleine could try for London again.

While he waited for a gap in the weather, Kleine concentrated on intensive training for his crews; many new men had arrived and were struggling with the demands and stresses of the bombing campaign. In London the population settled into the rhythm of the moon cycle, linking the arrival of the full moon with a return of the raiders, and as the time of the next full moon drew closer – 28 November – Londoners turned once more to the safety of the Underground stations. But good weather did not coincide and Kleine's men did not come. When they did finally return, in the early hours of 6 December, they did so under a new designation: Bombengeschwader 3 der OHL (Bogohl 3).

The moon was in its last quarter when Kleine received news of a break in the weather – meaning a very dark night by which to navigate. However, he grasped the opportunity and readied Bogohl 3, and for only the second time Rfa 501 joined the raid with two Staaken 'Giants'. Disappointed by the previous raid's failure to set London burning, this time the great majority of bombs loaded were incendiaries.

THE FAILURE OF THE FIRESTORM

The night of 5/6 December 1917 was freezing on the ground in London, there was frost and ice on windows, in the air the cold must have been almost unbearable. In Belgium 19 Gothas and two 'Giants' set course for England – three Gothas turned back early. The first crossed the Kent coastline at about 1.30am on 6 December and many of the raiding force targeted Kent with their bombs, including one of the 'Giants'. Later the other 'Giant' came inland but it too shied away from London. Although taken by surprise with the raid developing in the early hours of a dark morning, the RFC still put up 34 aircraft, including No. 39 squadron's two new high-performance Bristol Fighters, but no pilots located any enemy aircraft. The first of the six Gothas to penetrate the London defences approached the outer barrage at about 4.30am. When the first bombs began to fall at around 4.45am most Londoners were still asleep in their beds. About 40 incendiaries rained down across Westminster and Chelsea but just over half caused no damage at all, while the rest caused only minor damage. Two other curving, almost parallel, lines of incendiaries were dropped: one from Shaftesbury Avenue over Bloomsbury and Clerkenwell towards Hoxton, Bethnal Green and Mile End while the other followed a line from Somerset House in Aldwych up through Holborn, Farringdon, along Old Street, over Spitalfields and Whitechapel. These two bombing runs dropped about 90 incendiaries between them yet only three serious fires resulted. The most dramatic was just north of Liverpool Street Station, in Curtain Road at the junction with Worship Street. There a single bomb burnt out a cabinetmaker's factory and that of L. Rose and Co., producers of Rose's lime cordial. The London Fire Brigade estimated material damage caused by this fire at £45,400. A second serious conflagration occurred at 113 Whitechapel Road where the flames also engulfed a number of adjoining premises involved in the clothes

The wreckage of one of the two Gothas shot down in the early hours of 6 December 1917. One landed at Sturry near Canterbury, the other crashed on a golf course while attempting to land at Rochford airfield. All crew members survived.

Skeleton of Lower Right-hand Wing The Remains of the Fabric can be seen

Framework of Aileron or Balancing Flap

Framework of Aileron or Balancing Flap

Framework of Upper Left-h...

trade, causing damage estimated at £16,385. The third fire was at the Acorn Works in Henry Street (now Roger Street) off Grey's Inn Road. A bomb here set alight a range of buildings, recording damage estimated at £13,500.

Other bombing runs took place over south-west London (about 54 bombs: three explosive and 51 incendiary) in Lambeth, Kennington and Battersea as well as Clapham, Brixton and Balham, while in south-east London 68 bombs (nine explosive and 59 incendiaries) fell in Lewisham, Brockley, Sydenham, Dulwich and Lee. Despite dropping over 120 bombs south of the Thames the results were extremely limited. A fire at the Sunnybank Laundry by Vauxhall Park caused £2,000 of damage to the premises. Explosive bombs caused damage to a tenement in Burgoyne Road, Stockwell, while another landed in a garden in the inappropriately named Paradise Road, close to Stockwell station, injuring three children. The most deadly blast took place when a 50kg explosive bomb dropped in College Road, Dulwich. Here, at a property owned by the British Red Cross Society, the bomb exploded in a room where the caretaker's wife, Edith Howie, and her 13-year-old niece were sleeping, killing both. Her husband, who was in the kitchen at the time, reported that the 'force of the bomb was such as to blow my wife and the child through the roof.'

The barrage had once again given the German crews plenty to think about and for those inexperienced in the task often proved effective in turning them from their intended course. And for the first time it appears one of the London guns inflicted critical damage to a Gotha over the city. *The Times* reported that '... a series of shell-bursts culminated in one which apparently struck a raider. Loud cheers were raised, and cries of "Got him!" The enemy machine was seen to wobble and descend slowly to the north.'

Shrapnel peppered the Gotha, crewed by Leutnant S. R. Schulte, Leutnant P. W. Barnard and Vizefeldwebel B. Senf, damaging the port radiator. This gradually caused the engine to overheat and, once it caught fire, the crew knew they would have to try to land. They then came under fire from a mobile AA gun at Herne Bay and also a Lewis gun based at Bekesbourne airfield, which may have scored hits, but by then the damage was already done; the Gotha crash-landed in a field near Canterbury. The crew set fire to the wreckage of their aircraft and surrendered to a local special constable.

London Air Defence Area (LADA), September 1918

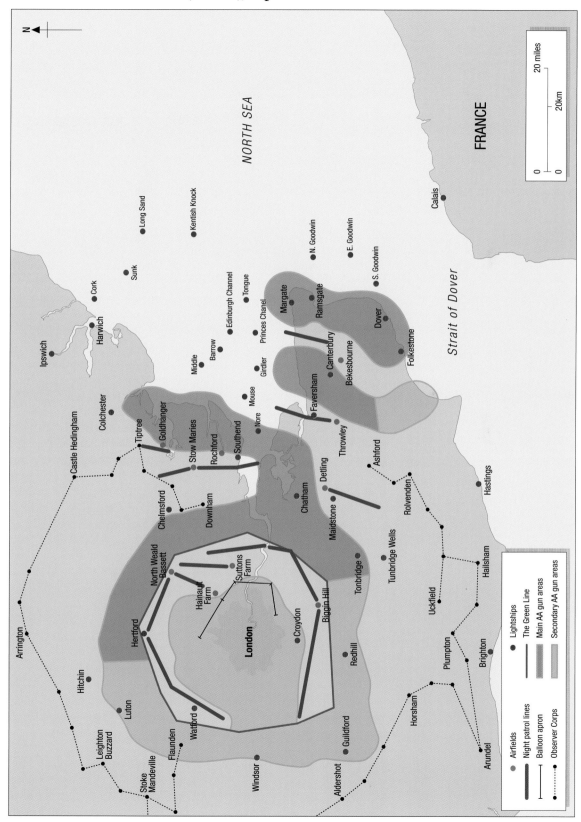

NORTH SEA

FRANCE

Strait of Dover

Calais

N. Goodwin
E. Goodwin
S. Goodwin

Long Sand
Kentish Knock

Sunk
Cork

Ipswich
Harwich

Margate
Ramsgate
Dover
Folkestone

Edinburgh Channel
Tongue
Princes Chanel
Girdler

Canterbury
Bekesbourne

Barrow
Middle
Mouse

Faversham
Throwley

Ashford

Hastings

Colchester

Castle Hedingham

Tiptree
Goldhanger
Stow Maries
Rochford
Southend
Nore

Detling
Chatham

Rolvenden

Chelmsford
Downham

Maldstone

Tunbridge Wells

Uckfield

Hailsham

North Weald
Bassett

Suttons
Farm

Tonbridge

Plumpton

Brighton

Arrington

Hainault
Farm

London

Croydon
Biggin Hill

Redhill

Horsham

Arundel

Hitchin

Hertford

Luton

Guildford

Aldershot

Leighton
Buzzard

Flaunden
Watford

Windsor

Stoke
Mandeville

20 miles
20km

0
0

Legend:

Airfields
Night patrol lines
Balloon apron
Observer Corps

Lightships
The Green Line
Main AA gun areas
Secondary AA gun areas

The single model R.IV-type Staaken 'Giant', the *R.12*, with its crew. Unlike the R.VI-type, which had four engines, the R.IV had six – two 160hp Mercedes D.III and four 220hp Benz Bz.IV – driving three propellers.

Another aircraft, a Gotha G.V, that failed to reach London, had a propeller shot away by AA gunfire while over Canvey Island, Essex. Looking for somewhere to land the pilot, Gemeiner J. Rzechtalski, steered towards the lights of Rochford airfield but they clipped a tree on their approach and crashed on a nearby golf course. The pilot and his fellow crew members, Leutnant R. Wessells and Vizfeldwebel O. Jakobs, crawled from the wreckage into the arms of their surprised captors. Later, when a group of officers was inspecting the wreck they lost a valuable prize when a signal pistol picked up by one went off accidentally and set the petrol-soaked wreck ablaze. Another Gotha failed to return, presumed forced down and lost at sea, while two more limped back and crash-landed in Belgium; a final aircraft crashed as it landed at its home airfield.

Kleine lost six of his 16 attacking aircraft, yet, despite dropping over 260 incendiary and 13 explosive bombs, total damage in the London area was estimated at £92,303 of which about half occurred at one site. The bombs killed two civilians and injured seven, while falling AA shells killed a man in Wanstead and injured eight others across London. Kleine's great hope to set London ablaze had failed. The problem was that so many of the incendiary bombs fell in roadways or gardens where they burnt out and those that did ignite could be extinguished by a determined person with water or sand if they could get to them early enough; others just failed to ignite. Ten years later, Major Hilmer von Bülow, a historian of the German air force wrote:

> A great deal of time was spent over the design of these incendiary bombs, on whose effect on the densely populated London area such high hopes were based. The bomb was a complete failure. During the two night raids on England, on the 31st of October and the 6th of December, 1917, large numbers of these bombs were dropped, both times with no success. The sound idea of creating panic and disorder by numbers of fires came to nothing owing to the inadequacy of the material employed.

In Germany technicians were working on a new foolproof incendiary bomb – the Elektron bomb – although it would not be ready for deployment until August 1918. But Hauptmann Rudolph Kleine was not to see it developed. Six days after the 6 December raid, Kleine led Bogohl 3 on a raid against British encampments near Ypres. Pounced upon by a patrol of No. 1 Squadron, RFC, Kleine's crew lost the battle; later a German soldier discovered Kleine's body on the ground, his Pour le Mérite still around his neck. The loss of Kleine did nothing to help the failing morale of Bogohl 3, already struggling with the constant attrition amongst its crews. Temporary command passed to Oberleutnant Richard Walter, Bogohl 3's senior flight commander.

A SUCCESS IN THE SKY

On Tuesday 18 December, after less than a week in command, forecasters alerted Walter to a break in the weather and, although his predecessors had relied on the light of the full moon, he took the opportunity and launched his first attack on this dark night. In London a thin mist hung over the Thames with the moon described as a 'thin sickle clear cut in an inky sky'. Fifteen Gothas set out on the raid with two dropping out before reaching England. On this occasion a single Staaken 'Giant' – the *R.12*, the single model of the R.IV type – also joined the raiding force. Reports estimate that six Gothas evaded the barrages and made it through to London, where bombing runs took place between 7.15 and 8.30pm. *R.12* reached the capital later, just after 9.00pm. With the unanticipated appearance of enemy aircraft on a dark night the warning system was caught off guard and notification of the imminent raid was received too late to send out warnings. The first bomb appears to have fallen on 187 Westminster Bridge Road, followed moments later by another on the Victoria Embankment, close to Cleopatra's Needle, just a short distance from where a previous bomb fell on 4 September.

The bomb killed three women and Henry King, a 38-year-old special constable, as they stood at a tram stop. An incendiary bomb landed on Murdoch's piano manufacturers at 91 Farringdon Road causing a huge fire. A further cluster fell close to the junction around King's Cross Road and Pentonville Road around 7.33pm, damaging over 120 houses, killing two children and injuring 22 civilians and a policeman before the aircraft flew out over Hackney Downs, where one final bomb dropped at about 7.45pm. A second aircraft followed a similar line, dropping bombs around Temple, Chancery Lane, Lincoln's Inn, Gray's Inn and ending the run over Kentish Town where it dropped three explosive bombs. Other bombs fell in Goswell Road, Aldersgate Street and a couple in Whitechapel. South of the Thames, a small cluster fell in Bermondsey and Walworth, with most damage occurring in Spa Road, Bermondsey, where four explosive bombs fell close together. Two of these caused extensive damage to buildings owned by the Salvation Army where people took shelter

The varying types of aerial bomb available to the German air force in 1918. From left to right: 50kg, 100kg, 300kg, 1,000kg, while the soldier in the centre holds a 12.5kg bomb.

Shrapnel damage visible to this day on the wall of 10 Stone Buildings, Lincoln's Inn, caused by a 50kg bomb that fell at about 8.05pm on 18 December. A small white disc set into the road shows where the bomb landed.

during the raids. A Mrs Gibbons who lived in the road rushed there with her five children and waited until '… a loud explosion occurred and the lights went out; the suspense was awful as we waited expecting the roof to fall in. In the midst of the confusion a voice shouted, "No lights! I'll shoot the first man to light a match!" We afterwards learned that a gas main had burst.'

Commander of the Gotha that bombed Bermondsey was Oberleutnant G. von Stachelsky, with Leutnant Friedrich Ketelsen and Gefreiter A. Weissmann as crew. It flew in over Essex where Captain G. W. Murlis Green, the commanding officer of No. 44 Squadron, closed in to attack, attracted by searchlights and the Gotha's two exhaust flares. His first attack failed when the muzzle flash from his guns temporarily blinded him. Ketelsen flew on and moments later Stachelsky began releasing his bombs over Bermondsey. With his night vision restored, Murlis Green made two more attempts to get into a position to attack, but although he reported his tracers entering the Gotha's fuselage, both times his muzzle-flash forced him away. Every time he attacked, caught in searchlights, he was targeted by Stachelsky with the front machine gun, but he commented that his adversary's 'tracers were always very wide of the mark'. He then closed in for a fourth attack, this time there was no searchlight. He emptied the rest of his ammunition drum into the Gotha at which point it dived steeply in front of him, and as he turned to get out of the way, he was caught in the slipstream, which sent his Sopwith Camel into a spin. By the time he regained control the Gotha had disappeared. But the bomber was in trouble. Bullets had damaged the starboard engine, which finally burst into flames halfway back to the coast. Ketelsen hoped to coax the Gotha back on one engine but it soon became clear that was impossible and he ditched in the sea off the coast at Folkestone at about 9.00pm. An armed trawler prepared to pick up the crew and with Stachelsky and Weissmann already safely on board, Ketelsen slipped from his precarious position on the upper wing and drowned.

While this drama played out, the final attack of the night began as 'Giant' *R.12* flew across London and dropped a huge 300kg bomb on Lyall Street, Belgravia. The bomb landed in the roadway gouging a great crater 30 by 20 by 7ft deep (9 x 6 x 2m). It damaged gas and water mains and about 20 houses

The 18 December 1917 raid

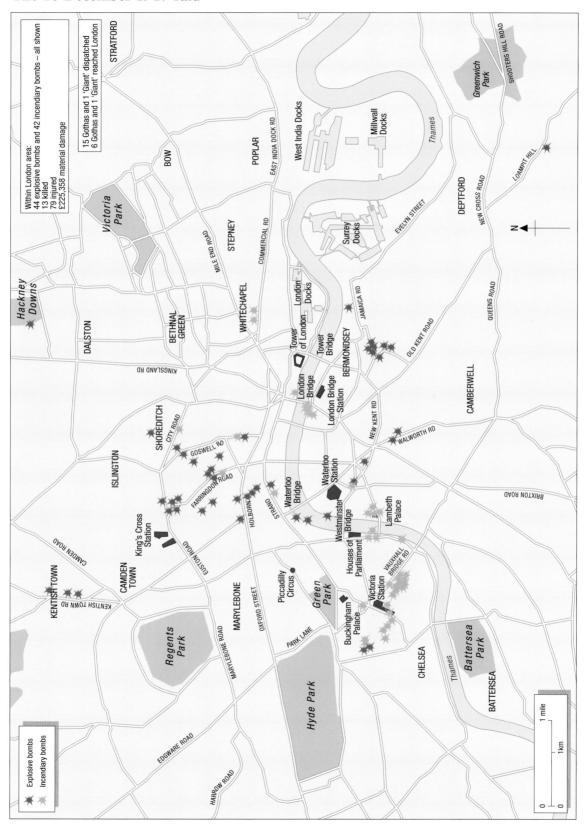

Within London area:
44 explosive bombs and 42 incendiary bombs – all shown
13 killed
79 injured
£225,358 material damage

15 Gothas and 1 'Giant' dispatched
6 Gothas and 1 'Giant' reached London

STRATFORD

Greenwich Park

SHOOTERS HILL ROAD

West India Docks

Millwall Docks

Thames

POPLAR

BOW

EAST INDIA DOCK RD

DEPTFORD

LOAMPIT HILL

NEW CROSS ROAD

Victoria Park

STEPNEY

MILE END ROAD

COMMERCIAL RD

Surrey Docks

EVELYN STREET

Hackney Downs

WHITECHAPEL

BETHNAL GREEN

London Docks

Tower of London

Tower Bridge

BERMONDSEY

JAMAICA RD

OLD KENT ROAD

QUEENS ROAD

CAMBERWELL

DALSTON

KINGSLAND RD

London Bridge

London Bridge Station

NEW KENT RD

SHOREDITCH

CITY ROAD

GOSWELL RD

WALWORTH RD

ISLINGTON

FARRINGDON ROAD

Waterloo Bridge

Waterloo Station

BRIXTON ROAD

HOLBORN

STRAND

King's Cross Station

EUSTON ROAD

Westminster Bridge

Lambeth Palace

KENTISH TOWN

CAMDEN ROAD

KENTISH TOWN RD

CAMDEN TOWN

MARYLEBONE

OXFORD STREET

Piccadilly Circus

Green Park

Houses of Parliament

VAUXHALL BRIDGE RD

Victoria Station

Regents Park

MARYLEBONE ROAD

PARK LANE

Buckingham Palace

CHELSEA

Battersea Park

Thames

BATTERSEA

Hyde Park

EDGWARE ROAD

HARROW ROAD

N

Explosive bombs
Incendiary bombs

1 mile

1km

0

0

The engineers' compartment in the nose of 'Giant' *R.12*, containing the two 160hp Mercedes engines. Unlike the R.VI-types, the R.IV had an open cockpit for the pilot which can be seen on the left.

close by, including breaking the windows of the Russian Embassy, but there were no casualties. It appears that the rest of the bomb load were incendiaries and these fell across Belgravia, Pimlico, Lambeth – where four bombs fell close to Lambeth Palace, residence of the Archbishop of Canterbury – and three dropped on or around Southwark Cathedral, but this resulted only in slight damage to the roof. The final incendiary bomb appears to have fallen on Billingsgate Fish Market where it caused a small fire.

A total of 43 explosive and 39 incendiary bombs were recorded falling on London, causing material damage estimated at £225,000, the largest single total since the Zeppelin raid of 8/9 September 1915 (£530,000). The final London casualty checks recorded 13 killed and 79 injured. But again, Bogohl 3 sustained heavy losses. With one Gotha confirmed shot down it was clear that the British defences were beginning to come to terms with the night-bomber raids. And back in Belgium the mournful toll continued: two Gothas were lost when they burst into flames on landing and five others sustained damage.

PREPARATIONS FOR A NEW YEAR

Yet Ashmore was not complacent and demanded improvements. The attack by Murlis Green had been the first recognized successful aerial engagement since the night raids began – one success from countless sorties. Two new Home Defence squadrons were forming to join the roster: Nos. 141 and 143. The balloon apron was extending although it never comprised the 20 sections originally envisaged; in the end there were just ten. Improvements in aerial gunnery followed: the new Neame gunsight included an illuminated ring that a Gotha filled at 100 yards' (90m) range and work was under way to eliminate the muzzle-flash causing pilots' temporary loss of night vision. A new bullet became available too for use in the Lewis gun – the RTS (Richard Threlfall and Sons) with explosive and incendiary capabilities. The aircraft available for Home

Defence improved too as more high-performance types such as the Sopwith Camel, Sopwith Pup, SE5a and the two-seater Bristol F.2B – the Bristol Fighter or 'Brisfit' – joined the squadrons, all capable opponents for the Gothas and 'Giants'.

The ground defences were overhauled too. A new system of anti-aircraft barrage fire superseded 'curtain' fire. The 'polygon' barrage aimed to surround enemy aircraft with shell bursts instead of presenting a line of fire across their path. Other improvements saw searchlights regrouped and their command system redefined while the observer posts of the Observer Corps, except those on the coast, passed to police control in December 1917. This was in reaction to concerns that those manning them consisted mainly of soldiers unfit for service overseas who in many cases lacked the alertness required for this vital role in the defence system. Demands for more aircraft followed too. At this point estimates showed that 89 day-fighters and 69 night-fighters defended London – although as some aircraft appeared in both sections the efficient strength was about 100 aircraft. Then, one final change followed. The raid on 18 December had caught the defences off guard, preventing the issue of an effective warning to the public. Angry scenes followed and in response the government granted the extension of the use of warning maroons. Previously authorized to warn only of daylight raids, now they could alert the public of the approach of hostile aircraft up to 11.00pm, although later alarms were permitted in instances where the police did not have enough warning to tour the streets with their placards.

While all this was under way Bogohl 3 and Rfa 501 waited impatiently for another chance to strike at London. However, London experienced an extremely cold January with thick blankets of fog wrapped protectively around the city. Back in Germany a new massive 1,000kg explosive bomb was ready, although only one 'Giant' was adapted to carry it, and intensive work continued to perfect the new Elektron incendiary bomb.

VI Brigade (Home Defence) – Royal Flying Corps – February 1918

No. 46 (Northern) Wing
No. 47 (South Midlands) Wing

(London Air Defence Wings)
No. 49 Wing
    No. 39 Sqn
    No. 44 Sqn
    No. 78 Sqn
    No. 141 Sqn

No. 50 Wing
    No. 37 Sqn
    No. 61 Sqn
    No. 75 Sqn
    No. 198 (Night Training) Sqn

No. 53 Wing
    No. 50 Sqn
    No. 61 Sqn
    No. 143 Sqn

THE 1918 RAIDS

THE LONG ACRE TRAGEDY

At last the sky looked clear again, and on Monday 28 January 1918 preparations for the first raid of the year were in full swing. But a change was coming and, after 13 Gothas had taken off in their now usual staggered pattern, fog closed in around the Belgian airfields and prevented the rest following. The fog extended far out to sea too, forcing six of the Gothas to turn back. Two 'Giants' joined the raid, but one soon turned back with engine trouble.

The Gothas crossed the coastline between 7.55 and 8.25pm, with just three attacking London. The other four settled for the less risky option of attacking coastal towns in north-east Kent. The night sky was clear and bright over London when, at about 8.00pm, the night-time air raid warning maroons exploded in the sky for the first time. In Shoreditch big queues were building up outside two music halls and a cinema for the evening performances. These sudden aerial explosions, which many presumed to be German bombs, took the crowds by surprise, causing a rush towards Bishopsgate railway goods yard which served as a vast air raid shelter. However, as the mass of people struggled to push through the narrow gates, panic set in. When order was finally restored the casualty list recorded 14 killed and 12 injured, crushed

The wreckage of Gotha G.V 938/16, brought down at Frund's Farm at Wickford in Essex on 28 January, following repeated attacks by two Sopwith Camels of No. 44 Squadron. All three of the crew died.

The 28/29 January 1918 raid

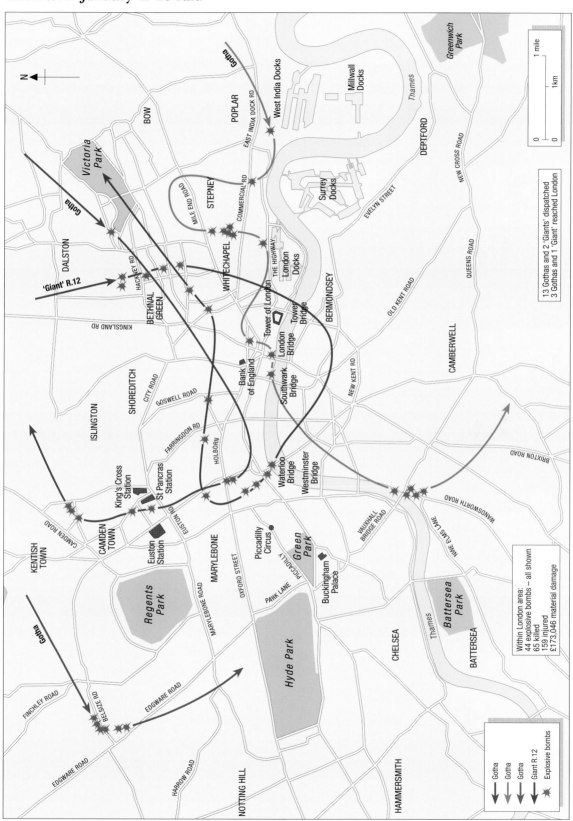

LEFT
Damage caused by the 100kg bomb that fell on Savoy Mansions, close to Victoria Embankment, early on 29 January. The Air Board had occupied the premises until the Air Ministry replaced that organization at the beginning of the month.

RIGHT
The devastation caused by the 300kg bomb dropped on Odhams Printing Works, Long Acre – an official air raid shelter. One of the huge printing presses has fallen through the floor and rolls of paper hang precariously on the upper floors. The tally of 38 killed and 85 wounded was the most caused in London by a single bomb.

and trampled in the press. A similar panic, at Mile End railway station, resulted in injuries to two women.

The first Gotha appeared over east London at about 8.45pm, having weaved its way through the defensive barrage and released a series of explosive bombs on Poplar, Limehouse and Stepney before passing over Shadwell and across the Thames by Cannon Street Station. It resumed bombing over Vauxhall where four bombs killed three men and injured three men, four women and three children.

Twenty minutes later a second Gotha appeared over London, dropping its first bomb at about 9.15pm in a garden in Gore Road, south Hackney, damaging eight houses. The next two bombs fell close together in Holborn causing considerable damage to a printworks before the aircraft turned northwards, dropping bombs close to Euston, King's Cross and St Pancras railway stations, with the last bomb dropping at 9.30pm.

For twenty minutes all was quiet but then, at about 9.50pm, a Gotha G.V, crewed by Leutnant Friedrich von Thomsen, and Unteroffiziere Karl Ziegler and Walter Heiden, appeared over north-west London and quickly unloaded six bombs on a curving line along Belsize Road towards Maida Vale, before turning eastwards and setting course for home. With a clear sky and a definite improvement in the coordination of London's defences, searchlights picked up the returning Gotha and, as it approached Romford, two No. 44 squadron Sopwith Camels, piloted by Captain G. H. Hackwill and 2nd Lieutenant C. C. Banks, observed its progress and turned to engage. A tremendous running battle developed between the three aircraft as the Camels swooped in to attack and then withdrew again, recovered their positions before attacking again – the whole drama watched closely from below. Then, as Banks turned away with mechanical problems, Hackwill made a fresh attack and this time he met with success – the Gotha shuddered, flames spread and the aircraft went down, crashing at Frund's Farm at Wickford in Essex (see artwork plate on pp. 70/71).

After this last Gotha turned away from London, just before 10.00pm, the guns fell silent over the city, and, although the all-clear did not sound, many took advantage of the lull and left the safety of the shelters to make their way home. However, London's ordeal was not yet over. *R.12*, the single R.IV-type Staaken 'Giant', crossed the coastline at about 10.25pm and after circling over Suffolk for some time was now heading towards London. Near Harlow a Bristol Fighter from No. 39 Squadron, flown by Lieutenant J. G. Goodyear and 1st AM W. T. Merchant, attacked *R.12* and, after a few ineffectual exchanges, bullets from one of *R.12*'s six or seven machine guns splattered along the Brisfit wounding Merchant in the arm and smashing the main petrol tank. With his engine stopped Goodyear turned away and expertly glided down to North Weald airfield to make a perfect landing.

Undeterred, *R.12* continued towards London, approaching the city at about 12.15am. The 'Giant' encountered heavy barrage fire but dropped its first bombs on Bethnal Green and Spitalfields, killing one and injuring 18, these bombs also demolishing three houses and damaging over 300. *R.12* then crossed the Thames and began turning until it recrossed the river by Waterloo Bridge where a bomb dropped in the river. The next smashed into Savoy Mansions causing considerable damage to the building; moments later bombs landed in the Flower Market at Covent Garden, Long Acre, Bedford Place and Hatton Garden before *R.12* dropped two last bombs on Bethnal Green and set course for home.

But it was the bomb that fell in Long Acre that left the most traumatic mark on London that night. The basement of Odhams Printing Works, a four-storey building in Long Acre with 10in. thick concrete floors on the two lower levels, was an official air raid shelter. People started arriving just after 8.00pm when the maroons fired their warning. The bomb dropped by *R.12* was a massive 300kg of high explosive; it missed the building but smashed through the pavement and exploded in one of the basement rooms. The blast shook the foundations and fire quickly spread through huge rolls of newsprint stored there. Some of those sheltering in the basement stumbled, bewildered, from the building as fire crews, policemen, ambulances and soldiers rushed to help. One woman, haunted by what she witnessed, recalled that 'there were shrieks and cries and blood and shattered walls and burning wood and bodies stretched on the floors'.

But as the rescuers began to pull people from the rubble, one of the outer walls gave way, collapsing inwards, and the weight falling on the heavy printing presses forced the floors to collapse and crush down on the basement. A boy, J. Sullivan, who had been in the shelter playing with two friends, was knocked unconscious by the first blast. His recollections tell of some of the horrors encountered by those who survived: '… when I regained my senses it was like a nightmare. Everything seemed to be alight and falling on me. I was pinned to the ground with a piece of machine across my legs. My two playmates were missing and no trace was ever found of them. I can vividly remember women and children, bleeding and burning, lying near me, and one woman with her dress blazing actually ran over me.'

The devastation was immense and the rubble so extensive that it was not until March, some six weeks later, that the last two bodies were recovered. The final toll was 38 killed (nine men, 19 women and ten children) and 85 injured (43 men, 28 women and 14 children), the most casualties caused by a single bomb on London during the war. Total casualties for the raid on the city amounted to 65 killed and 159 injured (nine of which were caused by anti-aircraft shells). As well as the Gotha shot down in Essex, Bogohl 3 also lost another four aircraft in landing accidents.

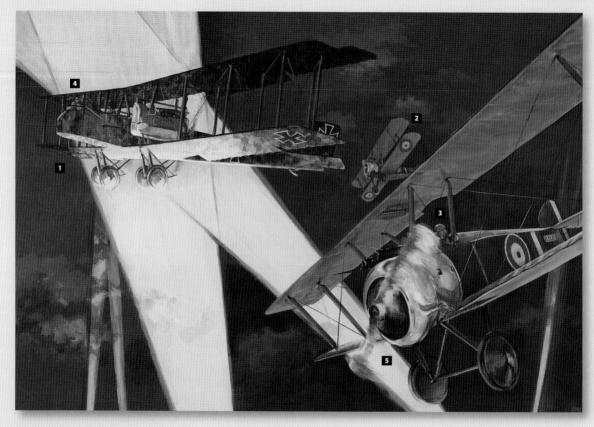

THE FIRST GOTHA SHOT DOWN ON BRITISH SOIL, MONDAY 28 JANUARY 1918 (pp. 70–71)

Having completed a bombing run over north-west London, Gotha G.V. 398/16 (shown in the irregular four-colour hand-painted night camouflage scheme (1)), crewed by Leutnant Friedrich von Thomsen, and Unteroffiziere Karl Ziegler and Walter Heiden, turned for home. Over Essex two pilots of No. 44 Squadron, based at Hainault, Captain George Hackwill (2) in Camel B2402 and 2nd Lieutenant Charles Banks (3), Camel B3827, observed the Gotha and turned to attack.

Many on the ground watched the combat develop as the Camels closed in on the Gotha at about 10,000ft (3,000m).

One swooped from above, crossed over the top of the raider and took up a position on his left behind and below but probably not more than 25 yards (23m) away. The other climbed up and got under the Gotha's tail. '… Tremendous machine-gun fire broke out immediately from all three machines. There was a succession of flashes as the guns blazed away…. Evidently he [the Gotha] did not like the situation, for early in the fight he made a sharp turn in an effort to get away, but the two British pilots kept a grip on him.'

At one point the Gotha appeared briefly to shake off its pursuers but then they were back; the Gotha 'fought hard (4)', but the British machines hung on, firing for all they were worth'. This running fight continued for about 10 miles (16km). Banks (5) then experienced some mechanical problems and turned away while Hackwill continued his attack. Then, as the report concluded, a burst from Hackwill hit the Gotha critically.

'A shot hit him in a vital spot and down he went. The machine had already started to burn, and it was obvious it was out of control.'

A farmer saw the aircraft fall as a 'bright ball of flame', crashing just 400 yards (366m) from his house. He ran to the spot '… and found it was a huge Gotha, well ablaze…. Within a few yards of the machine we could see by its light the charred body of a German, and two others were observed burning in the aeroplane.'

For their involvement in bringing down the first Gotha on British soil, both Hackwill and Banks received the Military Cross.

THE NIGHT OF THE 'GIANTS'

The following night, Tuesday 29 January, without support from Bogohl 3, Rfa 501 launched four of its 'Giants' against London alone. Only three – all of the R.VI-type – reached England: *R.25*, *R.26* and *R.39*. The last to cross the coastline was *R.26*, but having developed engine problems over Essex it returned to base. The first of the two remaining aircraft, *R.39*, came inland at about 10.05pm and encountered Captain A. Dennis, No. 37 Squadron, flying a BE12b. Dennis, flying at 12,000ft (3,650m) moved to 'fairly close range' and attacked. But after a furious exchange of fire, his aircraft became caught up in the 'Giant's' powerful slipstream and he lost sight of his adversary.

R.39 continued towards London after the engagement but it may have lost its bearings as it was over north-west London before it eventually turned southwards. Then, following a tortuous course over the south-western suburbs it appeared over the Old Deer Park, Richmond and Syon Park at about 11.30pm, dropping 16 incendiary and two explosive bombs which caused little or no damage. *R.39* then turned east and began dropping an extended string of explosive bombs. The first, tragically, demolished a house in Whitestile Road, Brentford. George Bentley was on his way home when he '… saw an aeroplane caught in the beam of a searchlight. At the same moment a man a few yards in front of me dived to the ground and shouted to me to lie down, which I did…. There were three deafening thuds and flashes.'

Bentley rushed to his house, which had suffered in the blast, but, finding his family were uninjured, he then ran to Whitestile Road where he discovered that the bomb had hit a friend's house. As he stared at the devastation he heard a groan. Bentley clambered over the rubble, then, he later recalled: 'I pulled and wriggled my way into the cellar, which was full of gas and water, and in the darkness came across a young woman, only just alive. Most of her clothes were blown off her. With help I managed to get her to the surface, but by that time she was dead.'

The next morning the bodies of the wife of Bentley's friend, who was away serving as a sergeant in the Middlesex Regiment, and an elderly woman were also recovered from the wreckage along with those of five of his children.

LEFT
This superb photo shows Staaken 'Giant' *R.39* – an R.VI-type – at Scheldewindeke, with *R.25* in the background. *R.39*, commanded by the leader of Rfa 501, Hauptmann Richard von Bentivegni, was the only aircraft raiding England adapted to carry the 1,000kg bomb. (Collection DEHLA)

RIGHT
Oberleutnant Hans-Joachim von Seydlitz-Gerstenberg, commander of Staaken 'Giant' *R.12* with a 300kg bomb bearing the inscription 'K.V. Für London' – K.V. = *Kriegsverwendungsfähige* (fit for active service). (IWM Q 108842)

After the bombs on Brentford, *R.39* dumped eight in close concentration on the Metropolitan Water Board Works by Kew Bridge on the north bank of the River Thames. These bombs caused considerable damage in the area and claimed the lives of two men at the waterworks. Another two dropped in Chiswick High Road damaging 72 houses before the last fell in Park Road, Chiswick, after which *R.39* crossed the Thames and took a homeward course south of the river. Three RFC pilots attempted to engage the returning 'Giant' but it shrugged off all their attacks.

The other 'Giant' to reach London, *R.25*, came inland at about 10.50pm. The crew brushed off an attack from a No. 37 Squadron BE2e and then, 20 minutes later, a Sopwith Camel of No. 44 squadron observed *R.25* near North Benfleet and attacked. The pilot, 2nd Lieutenant R. N. Hall, tried to close in but every time he did his guns jammed. Another pilot from the squadron, 2nd Lieutenant H. A. Edwardes, joined the attack and fired three bursts before his guns jammed; selflessly he then switched on his fuselage light and flew above the 'Giant' to attract other pilots. *R.25* 'kept turning sharply to the left and right losing height' as it continued towards London. Two more No. 44 Squadron pilots attacked: 2nd Lieutenant T. M. O'Neill and squadron commander Major G. W. Murlis Green. O'Neill experienced frustrating problems with his guns as he attacked before losing *R.25* in the dark, while Murlis Green, thwarted at first by the 'short and accurate bursts' of machine-gun fire aimed at him, eventually got below the 'Giant's' tail and opened fire at what he believed was 50 yards' (45m) range. However, confusion caused by the Neame gunsight meant that he later discovered the range was far greater. Pilots knew that a Gotha filled the gunsight ring at 100 yards (90m), but little was yet known about the 'Giants'; at almost twice the size of a Gotha, a 'Giant' was much further away when it filled the ring. Murlis Green reported later that, '... all my R.T.S. [ammunition] looked as if it was detonating on the fuselage of the hostile machine. I kept my triggers pressed and fired one complete double drum of R.T.S. and three quarters of a drum from my second gun. At any moment I expected the hostile machine to burst into flames.'

But *R.25* continued on its course. When Murlis Green later discussed the incident with his pilots they informed him that his bullets were bursting prematurely, at about 100 yards (90m), still short of the target.

This whole experience however must have been sobering for the crew of *R.25* for next, with horror, they saw one of the balloon aprons looming up directly ahead. They turned sharply away, released their entire load of 20 explosive bombs over Wanstead shortly after midnight, where they caused negligible damage, and turned for home. Having landed safely back in Belgium the much-relieved and fortunate crew of *R.25* discovered 88 bullet holes in their aircraft.

CHELSEA – THE 1,000KG BOMB

In February, Bogohl 3 welcomed back their former commander Ernst Brandenburg after a period of convalescence following his crash just over seven months earlier. Now walking with difficulty on an artificial leg, he found his former command much demoralized by the regular loses they were experiencing, particularly in landing accidents. He immediately suspended any further action by Bogohl 3 and ordered replacement aircraft to return the squadron to full strength.

On 16 February at about 10.10pm *R.39* dropped its single 1,000kg bomb on the north-east wing of the Royal Hospital, Chelsea. The bomb killed five, injured three, destroyed three buildings within the hospital grounds, severely damaged another and caused slight damage to another 200 buildings close by.

Therefore, when the next air raid set out on the evening of 16 February, the pilots of Rfa 501 continued the assault on London alone. Five 'Giants' set out but, encountering strong winds, three switched to the secondary target of Dover, leaving just the more powerfully engined *R.12* and *R.39* to continue towards London. On board *R.39* hung a single bomb; weighing 1,000kg, it was 13ft (4m) long and the heaviest type dropped from the air during the war.

The two crossed the coast around 9.40pm with *R.12* flying a few minutes ahead. At about 10.15pm, *R.12*, commanded by Oberleutnant Hans-Joachim von Seydlitz-Gerstenberg and piloted by Leutnant Götte, was approaching Woolwich in south-east London at a height of 9,500ft (2,900m) when suddenly before them loomed a section of the balloon apron. Götte made a desperate attempt to avoid the steel cables but his starboard wing made contact and threw *R.12* dramatically to the right before it fell out of control to the left. With immense coolness Götte throttled down all engines then opened up the two port engines which allowed him, after plummeting 1,000ft (300m), to regain control and steer away to the south-west. During those anxious moments one of the mechanics saved himself from being thrown out of his engine nacelle only by holding on to the forward exhaust manifold, severely burning his hands. The violent manoeuvres shook free two 300kg bombs which exploded in Woolwich. One demolished a building in Artillery Place, killing five and injuring two, the other blasted a great crater in the road by the parade ground of the Royal Artillery Barracks and damaged St George's Garrison Church; it also killed a nurse and an Australian soldier. A quick inspection of *R.12* showed that the encounter with the balloon apron, although no doubt terrifying for the crew, had inflicted only minor damage to the aircraft so they turned over Beckenham, offloaded their remaining eight bombs and turned for home.

The bombs fell in a group near Shortlands railway station causing only minor damage in the vicinity.

The leader of Rfa 501, Richard von Bentivegni, commanded *R.39*, now specially adapted to carry a single massive 1,000kg bomb. He believed he dropped the bomb east of the City but it actually fell in Chelsea, on the north-east wing of the Royal Hospital, home of the Chelsea Pensioners. The bomb killed an officer of the hospital staff and four of his family, but rescuers discovered three children still alive beneath the rubble and debris of the blast.

The dark moonless night aided the two 'Giants' on their way home and although 60 defensive sorties were flown that night there were only three brief sightings. All returned in one piece although *R.33*, one of those forced back early, limped home on one engine.

'A FINE PIECE OF SHOOTING'

Despite having only one aircraft available after the experiences of the previous night, Bentivegni ordered *R.25* – one of the R.VI-types – to raid London alone on 17 February. *R.25* came inland at about 9.45pm and managed to avoid the attention of the RFC on the inward journey, but encountered a stiff barrage fire from the AA guns near Gravesend, Kent. Taking evasive action, *R.25* circled around before dropping an incendiary bomb on Slade Green near Erith. Then it continued over Bexley and Eltham before dropping the first of its 19 explosive bombs, on Newstead Road, Lee, and left an evenly spaced trail of destruction right across London, with bombs falling in Hither Green, Lewisham, New Cross, Peckham, Camberwell, Southwark, New Fetter Lane in the City, Holborn and ending, devastatingly, on St Pancras Station. Such was the accuracy of the bombing run that a British analysis of the raid was generous in its praise of the tight grouping of five bombs on the station, describing it as '… by far the most accurate and concentrated fire ever yet brought to bear on any target in London, either by day or night and was a fine piece of shooting by the man responsible for it.' This achievement is often attributed to Leutnant Max Borchers, however, the credit is due to Hans-Wolf Fleischhauer.

On the night of 17 February 'Giant' *R.25* – an R.VI type – made a solo raid on London. The accurate concentration of five bombs on St Pancras Station brought technical appreciation from a British observer who described it as 'a fine piece of shooting'.

Here a Bristol Fighter and SE5a (below) take part in a flying display at the Shuttleworth Collection. Captain Cecil Lewis (author of *Sagittarius Rising*), No. 61 Squadron, was flying an SE5a on 17 February 1918 when twice attacked over Essex by 'friendly fire'.

Yet beyond this professional appreciation lay the personal tragedies of the raid. The first 12 bombs caused varying levels of damage to hundreds of properties, killed a soldier home on leave in Searlees Road, Southwark, and injured eight other people.

However, the situation at St Pancras was entirely different. The five bombs fell within seconds of one another on the station and adjoining Midland Hotel. One of the bombs struck a tower of the hotel sending heavy masonry crashing down through the building and three exploded on the station. The two that claimed most casualties landed either side of an archway leading through to the platforms where the double blast killed a number of people taking shelter from the raid.

A nurse, one of the first rescuers to arrive, reached the archway that had taken the blast: 'About ten bodies lay there, terribly mutilated; and two or three soldiers must have been among the victims, for we found two caps, three swagger canes and a limb with a puttee on it – all that remained of them, so far as I could see.'

Others had lucky escapes. A family staying in the Midland Hotel sought shelter and eventually found themselves, with others, down in the coal bay of the hotel. Then a terrific crash followed by darkness. One of the family recalled that '… showers of splintering glass fell around us, and coal dust fell, it seemed, by the ton. Those of us who were not lying on the ground bleeding and groaning were practically choking.… How long we stayed like that I do not know.'

Eventually rescued, as they staggered from the darkened coal bay a grisly spectacle confronted them: 'When we moved we seemed to be ankle-deep in broken glass; and as we left the ruins matches flickered, and in their light a ghastly sight met our eyes. Dead and injured lay everywhere.… Picking our way carefully, we at last came out into the air, to see in the distance flames leaping up to the sky.'

Within the station and hotel the final toll reached 20 killed (including one soldier) and 22 injured (including five soldiers, a sailor and a policeman).

The RFC had 69 aircraft in the sky searching for *R.25*, but the great noise generated by the aircraft's engines caused wildly conflicting accounts of numbers of enemy aircraft and their position. More than one of the aircraft on patrol found themselves subject to 'friendly fire'. Captain C. A. Lewis of No. 61

The 17 February and 7/8 March 1918 raids

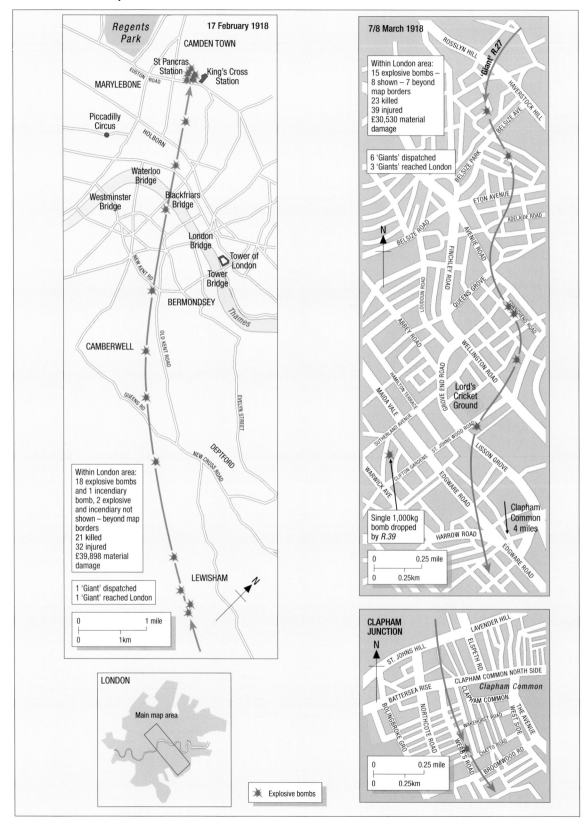

17 February 1918

Regents Park

CAMDEN TOWN

St Pancras Station

King's Cross Station

MARYLEBONE

EUSTON ROAD

Piccadilly Circus

HOLBORN

Waterloo Bridge

Westminster Bridge

Blackfriars Bridge

NEW KENT RD

London Bridge

Tower of London

Tower Bridge

BERMONDSEY

Thames

CAMBERWELL

OLD KENT ROAD

QUEENS RD

EVELYN STREET

DEPTFORD

NEW CROSS ROAD

Within London area:
18 explosive bombs and 1 incendiary bomb, 2 explosive and incendiary not shown – beyond map borders
21 killed
32 injured
£39,898 material damage

1 'Giant' dispatched
1 'Giant' reached London

LEWISHAM

N

0 _____ 1 mile
0 _____ 1km

LONDON

Main map area

Explosive bombs

7/8 March 1918

ROSSLYN HILL

Giant R.27

HAVERSTOCK HILL

BELSIZE AVE

Within London area:
15 explosive bombs –
8 shown – 7 beyond map borders
23 killed
39 injured
£30,530 material damage

6 'Giants' dispatched
3 'Giants' reached London

BELSIZE PARK

ETON AVENUE

ADELAIDE ROAD

N

BELSIZE ROAD

AVENUE ROAD

FINCHLEY ROAD

LONDON ROAD

QUEENS GROVE

TOWNSHEND ROAD

ABBEY ROAD

HAMILTON TERRACE

GROVE END ROAD

WELLINGTON ROAD

Lord's Cricket Ground

MAIDA VALE

SUTHERLAND AVENUE

CLIFTON GARDENS

ST. JOHNS WOOD ROAD

LISSON GROVE

WARWICK AVE

EDGWARE ROAD

Clapham Common 4 miles

Single 1,000kg bomb dropped by R.39

HARROW ROAD

EDGWARE ROAD

0 _____ 0.25 mile
0 _____ 0.25km

CLAPHAM JUNCTION

N

LAVENDER HILL

ST. JOHNS HILL

ELSPETH RD

CLAPHAM COMMON NORTH SIDE

Clapham Common

BATTERSEA RISE

BOLINGBROKE GRO

NORTHCOTE ROAD

CLAPHAM COMMON

THE AVENUE

WEST SIDE

WAKEHURST ROAD

WEBB'S ROAD

CHATTO ROAD

BROOMWOOD ROAD

0 _____ 0.25 mile
0 _____ 0.25km

Squadron, took it in his stride. In his report he wrote 'Several times I was caught in searchlight beams and over Benfleet was fired at. Shooting very good. Burst exactly at my height (11,000 feet) and put several holes in my machine.'

Later that patrol another RFC pilot attacked Lewis. Unfazed, he added, 'Judging the machine had made a mistake I put my machine into a spin and cleared'.

The extremely cool commander of *R.25* was quick to realize the costly effect his solo raid had on the British defences. The London guns alone fired off about 3,800 shells; in his report he wrote 'An attack by a single [Giant] is sufficient to alert the entire British defence system and to cause the expenditure of vast quantities of ammunition. It is seemingly from nervousness that not only anti-aircraft guns in the vicinity of the aircraft but also some 30km distant were being fired blindly into the air.'

Such was the nervous state of the British defences that a full-scale false alarm took place on the following night – 18 February – with 55 defensive sorties flown by the RFC and thousands of shells blasted aimlessly into the sky. In fact, the raiders did not return for almost three weeks.

THE AURORA BOREALIS RAID

Up until now, the aircraft of Rfa 501 had occupied the airfield at Sint-Denijs-Westrem, formally home airfield of Kasta 13 and 14 of Kagohl 3, and still the base for Armeeflugpark Nr. 4, but on 7 March Rfa 501 moved to a new airfield at Scheldewindeke, south of Ghent. It is surprising therefore, amidst the bustle of the move and on a moonless night, that Bentivegni ordered a raid that same evening.

The terrible destruction caused by the 1,000kg bomb dropped by *R.39* on Warrington Crescent, Maida Vale. Amongst the 12 killed in the blast was Lena Ford, who, in 1914, wrote the lyrics for Ivor Novello's hugely popular wartime song, 'Keep The Home Fires Burning'.

Six 'Giants' took off, one dropped out leaving five to carry out the raid, but only three attacked London: *R.13* – the single R.V type – and two R.VI types, *R.27* and *R.39*. Again, *R.39* carried a single 1,000kg bomb. The crews found navigation difficult that night. Hauptmann Arthur Schoeller, commanding *R.27*, left a fascinating report of the raid: 'We approach the coast; the night is so dark that the coastline below us is but a mere suggestion. Under us is a black abyss, no waves are seen, no lights of surface vessels flicker as we head for the Thames estuary at Margate. On our right, in the distant north, is our only light, the weak pulsating glow of the aurora borealis. Ahead of us a black nothingness.'

As the aircraft progressed clouds developed and thickened and it was only when searchlights illuminated the clouds below that Schoeller realized he was over England.

Requesting wireless bearings he discovered he was south-east of London so he turned towards the city, crossed the Thames and, turning southwards over Hampstead, released his bombs just after midnight. The first two fell in the Belsize Park area, followed by three more in St John's Wood. There a bomb on New Street (now Newcourt Street) demolished two houses, killing two families, before another exploded in the road outside Lord's Cricket Ground. Here the blast killed a soldier of the Royal Horse Artillery and Lieutenant-Colonel F. H. A. Wollaston, Rifle Brigade, who was on leave from service in Palestine.

R.27 continued south, crossed back over the Thames, circled in the face of heavy AA fire, then, having one more devastating blow to land, dropped a 100kg bomb in Burland Road, just west of Clapham Common. A mother and daughter heard the bomb explode:

> ... there was a dreadful shriek through the air and a terrible thud. A big bomb had landed in the middle of the road. It took the front of four houses clean out, ours being one. My mother had to shake me to make me speak. It just seemed as if we were waiting for the end. Mess, and pandemonium; water rushing everywhere, and the smell of gas, for it had hit the main, and there was a great flame in the road.

R.27 headed home, but with the Belgian coast in sight all four engines seized. A quick investigation revealed that the fuel lines had frozen because of 'water-contaminated gasoline'. Too late to thaw them, Schoeller realized he must crash, but thanks to the great gliding capabilities of the 'Giant' he managed to reach land. Then, using flares to illuminate the ground below, all he could see were trenches and hollows. Considering his options, Schoeller determined his best action, aware that if he hit any obstacle he risked annihilation: 'Therefore, by pulling sharply on the controls I stall the aircraft letting it fall almost vertically against the ground. With a mighty impact it hits in front of a wide ditch. The right landing gear collapses and the right lower wing shatters, but no crew member is injured.'

Another aircraft, one of those that did not reach London and believed to be *R.36*, also made an emergency landing in Belgium and was wrecked.

Back in London, as *R.27* commenced its bombing run, *R.39*, carrying the single 1,000kg bomb had already completed its mission. The recipient of this steel-encased metric ton of destruction was Warrington Crescent, a quiet residential street in Maida Vale, just over half a mile from Paddington Station.

The Reverend William Kilshaw, living half a mile away, was sheltering in his basement listening to 'the barking of the anti-aircraft guns' as the clock approached midnight: 'Suddenly the darkness of the room was broken in upon by a vivid flash… and a terrific roar caused the whole house to tremble. Our top window panes fell to the ground with a shattering noise…. After the bombardment we cautiously went to the window, to behold a scene reminiscent of what one reads of the Great Fire of London. The sky to the east was lurid with flames, in which dense smoke poured: the smitten district was afire.'

The bomb smashed through the roof and dividing wall between Nos. 63 and 65, four-storey Victorian houses, and detonated inside. The blast destroyed the two buildings and the two adjoining. The houses, 'all solidly built, were utterly wrecked, the four houses reduced to hideous piles of wreckage'. The bomb also caused serious damage to another 20 buildings and slight damage to 400 in the surrounding area. It took a number of days before all the bodies were accounted for, the final tally reaching 12 killed and 33 injured.

The third of the 'Giants' to reach London, *R.13*, encountered engine problems as it approached London from the north after midnight. Bombs fell in fields north of Golders Green, at Mill Hill and Whetstone. The last of these exploded at about 12.30am in a garden in Totteridge Lane causing severe damage to houses close by, killing a man and injuring three men, six women and a child. In all, 157 buildings were damaged before *R.13* turned away and the crew nursed it home on three of its five engines.

Although the RFC flew 42 defensive sorties, less than previous raids due to mist over some of the more eastern airfields, there were no sightings of Rfa 501's raiding aircraft. The evening ended tragically for the RFC when Captain A. B. Kynoch, No. 37 Squadron, flying a BE12, and Captain H. C. Stroud, No. 61 Squadron, in an SE5a, collided over Rayleigh, Essex, resulting in the deaths of both pilots.

THE AGONY OF THE 'GIANTS'

London readied itself for the next raid, a raid that people now feared could come at any stage of the moon. However, the skies over London remained empty for the rest of the week, then the month, and the next month too. The reason for the lack of enemy activity over London was the launch of the German army's massive spring offensive, the 'Kaiserschlacht', on the Western Front on 21 March 1918; the Army needed all squadrons to support the great advance. It was not until May, after the push to the Channel ports ground to a halt that attention turned back to London. Then, the largest raid of the war set out for the capital, but not before another night of great loss for the German raiders.

Bentivegni planned a raid with Rfa 501 for the night of 9 May and Brandenburg was keen to launch Bogohl 3 too. However, Brandenburg's weather officer predicted heavy fog that night and advised against it. Brandenburg heeded the advice and duly informed Bentivegni, but the commander of Rfa 501, determined to the point of recklessness, ignored the advice and went ahead.

The weather forecast proved accurate and with fog closing in the four 'Giants' were recalled to Scheldewindeke. Although fog now completely smothered the airfield, the returning aircraft ignored advice to fly to alternate sites and all tried to land anyway. *R.32* crashed and exploded on landing and all but one of the crew was killed. *R.26* flew into the ground whereupon it burst into flames, again with only one survivor and *R.29* was wrecked when it hit some trees; fortunately the crew survived. Only *R.39*, with Bentivegni on board, managed a successful landing.

Leutnant Georgii (centre), Bogohl 3's weather officer on the roof of the University of Ghent supervising the release of a meteorological balloon. At times, both Kleine and Rfa 501's commander, Bentivegni, ignored his advice. (IWM Q 73546)

THE WHITSUN RAID

The population of London was enjoying a pleasant Whitsun Bank Holiday weekend on Sunday 19 May 1918. Good weather and an absence of German bombers in the skies over the city for ten weeks promoted a relaxed mood. The skies over London that night were clear while 'a lazy breeze scarcely rustled the young leaves of the trees in the garden squares'. Into this peaceful night Germany launched its largest air raid of the war.

While Bogohl 3 focused on bombing missions on the Western Front, Brandenburg always watched for favourable weather over England. The report he wanted finally arrived on 19 May and he wasted no time in preparing 38 Gothas for the raid; this time two single-seater Rumpler aircraft led the way to check the weather ahead. Elsewhere, following the disaster earlier in the month, Bentivegni could add only three 'Giants' to this great aerial armada.

Reassured that the weather ahead was clear, the first of the Gothas came inland over the north Kent coast just after 10.30pm, the last appeared around midnight. As with previous raids a number of aircraft were forced to turn back and it appears that 28 Gothas and the three 'Giants' made it inland. Reports from observer posts all over the south-east swamped LADA headquarters, stretching the telephone system to the limit. For the first time aircraft of the recently amalgamated Royal Air Force took off to oppose the raiders; they flew 88 sorties and soon the skies over Kent and Essex buzzed like a hornets' nest.

Captain C. J. Q. Brand, No. 112 Squadron, took off at 11.15pm in a Sopwith Camel and, attracted by searchlight activity, quickly spotted the exhaust flares of a westbound Gotha over Faversham. The Gotha opened up with its machine guns as Brand closed to 50 yards (45m) and fired two 20-round bursts from his own guns in return, hitting and stopping the Gotha's starboard engine. The Gotha, crewed by Oberleutnant R. Bartikowski and Vizefeldwebels F. Bloch and H. Heilgers, turned sharply to the north-east and attempted to evade the attack while losing height. Then Brand '... Followed

The 19/20 May 1918 raid

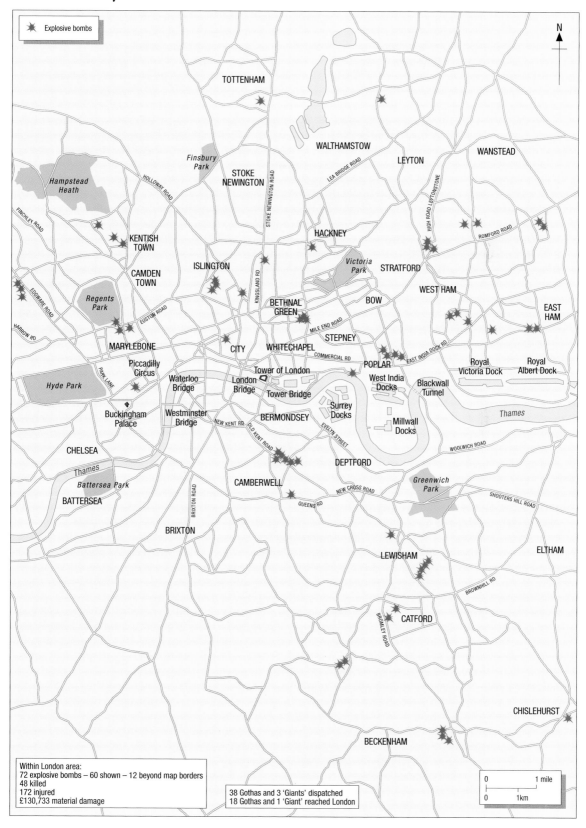

Explosive bombs

N

TOTTENHAM

WALTHAMSTOW

LEYTON

WANSTEAD

Finsbury Park

STOKE NEWINGTON

HACKNEY

STRATFORD

Hampstead Heath

HOLLOWAY ROAD

STOKE NEWINGTON ROAD

LEA BRIDGE ROAD

HIGH ROAD LEYTONSTONE

ROMFORD ROAD

FINCHLEY ROAD

KENTISH TOWN

CAMDEN TOWN

ISLINGTON

Victoria Park

WEST HAM

EAST HAM

EDGWARE ROAD

Regents Park

KINGSLAND RD

BETHNAL GREEN

BOW

HARROW RD

EUSTON ROAD

PARK LANE

MARYLEBONE

CITY

WHITECHAPEL

STEPNEY

MILE END ROAD

COMMERCIAL RD

POPLAR

EAST INDIA DOCK RD

Royal Victoria Dock

Royal Albert Dock

Hyde Park

Piccadilly Circus

Waterloo Bridge

Tower of London

London Bridge

Tower Bridge

West India Docks

Blackwall Tunnel

Thames

Buckingham Palace

Westminster Bridge

NEW KENT RD

OLD KENT ROAD

BERMONDSEY

Surrey Docks

EVELYN STREET

Millwall Docks

WOOLWICH ROAD

CHELSEA

Thames

Battersea Park

BATTERSEA

BRIXTON ROAD

CAMBERWELL

DEPTFORD

NEW CROSS ROAD

QUEENS RD

Greenwich Park

SHOOTERS HILL ROAD

BRIXTON

LEWISHAM

ELTHAM

BROWNHILL RD

BROMLEY ROAD

CATFORD

CHISLEHURST

BECKENHAM

Within London area:
72 explosive bombs – 60 shown – 12 beyond map borders
48 killed
172 injured
£130,733 material damage

38 Gothas and 3 'Giants' dispatched
18 Gothas and 1 'Giant' reached London

0   1 mile

0   1km

E.A [enemy aircraft] down and closed to 25 yards and fired three bursts of about 25 rounds each. E.A. burst into flames and fell to pieces'.

Although the flames from the burning Gotha enveloped his Camel and scorched his face and moustache, Brand followed the burning wreck down to 3,000ft (900m) until he saw it crash on the Isle of Sheppey at 11.26pm, just 11 minutes after he had taken off.

The AA guns along the Thames Estuary were pounding the skies too and it appears only 18 aircraft battled their way through the barrage, the rest repulsed by the onslaught. The Metropolitan Police recorded 72 explosive bombs over a wide area, with just a handful landing in the central area, roughly grouped as follows.

11.30pm	Catford, Sydenham, Bexley, Bexleyheath
11.40pm	Poplar, Walthamstow, Sidcup
11.45pm	St James's, Bethnal Green, Tottenham, Manor Park
11.50pm	Lewisham, Bromley
11.55pm	Old Kent Road, Rotherhithe, Kilburn
12.00am	Forest Gate, Stratford, Peckham, Bexleyheath, Chislehurst
12.10am	Hither Green, Lewisham, Lee, Islington, Kentish Town
12.15am	Kentish Town, Gospel Oak, Limehouse
12.20am	Regent's Park, Marylebone, West Ham, East Ham, Plaistow, Canning Town
12.30am	City, Shoreditch, Hackney, East Ham, Barking
12.40am	Dalston

The most casualties that night caused by a single bomb were in Sydenham where a 100kg bomb fell in Sydenham Road. The bomb demolished two houses, which incorporated a dairy and bakery, as well as damaging 46 others, claiming the lives of 18 and injuring 14. These casualty figures include three soldiers killed and another 12 injured, all part of a motor transport depot billeted in buildings opposite where the bomb fell. A former soldier of the Royal Army Medical Corps, P. Leach, was one of the first on the scene and thought the scene that confronted him 'like a battlefield afterwards, with the dead and dying: and there were civilians lying dead in the gutter'. Having torn up sheets to make bandages he got to work: 'I found a Sergeant Oliver with his leg crushed to pulp, and I attended to him first. Others were getting the dead out of the shops. Then I attended to one little mite of a girl who had lost both of her feet.'

About 15 minutes later three bombs landed close together in Bethnal Green. Two fell on the premises of Allen & Hanbury, wholesale chemist and druggist, and one in neighbouring Corfield Street. The three bombs claimed the lives of a man and two women as well as injuring seven men, eight women and two children while causing massive damage; a third of the factory was destroyed, 14 houses seriously damaged and 227 suffered minor damage. Total casualties in London that night amounted to 48 killed and 172 injured. But the bombers, having spent as little time as possible over London, then faced a return journey fraught with danger. That night the LADA guns fired over 30,000 rounds skywards.

A No. 39 Squadron Bristol Fighter caught a Gotha flying at 10,000ft (3,000m) north of Hainault, at about 12.05am. Following a running fight the Gotha smashed into the ground on open land on the outskirts of East Ham. (See the artwork plate on pp. 86/87.)

Elsewhere Major F. Sowrey, No. 143 Squadron, who had previously shot down a Zeppelin in September 1916, engaged a Gotha V at about 12.25am returning from bombing Peckham and Rotherhithe. Flying an SE5a, Sowrey closed and fired off two drums of Lewis gun ammunition and, despite the Gotha's evasive tactics, closed again to open with his Vickers. But an engine stall caused a spin and by the time he recovered control Sowrey had lost sight of the Gotha – but it appears he had wounded the pilot, Vizefeldwebel Albrecht Sachtler. Doubtful of reaching Belgium the crew began searching for somewhere to land when a Bristol Fighter of No. 141 Squadron, crewed by Lieutenants Edward Turner and Henry Barwise, pounced on the struggling Gotha. The first burst, fired by the observer Barwise hit the Gotha's port engine as it was attempting to reach the illuminated landing ground at Frinsted, Kent. Attacked again, the Gotha dived, defending itself by firing its rear gun in short bursts at the Brisfit. Then Barwise's gun jammed and, encountering engine problems, Turner pulled away and gave up the attack. However, the Gotha was now in a bad way and despite Sachtler's best efforts it crashed between Frinsted and Harrietsham at about 12.45am. Only the rear gunner, Unteroffizier Hermann Tasche, who suffered a broken arm, survived the landing.

A fourth Gotha met with disaster near Clacton after the pilot came down low to clear cloud cover in an attempt to establish its position. An engine

Another shot of a crashed Gotha, probably the same aircraft as in the previous illustration – the small arrow indicating an unexploded 50kg bomb with its nose buried in the ground. (C. Ablett)

THE LARGEST, AND LAST, RAID OF THE WAR, 19/20 MAY 1918 (pp. 86–87)

After a gap of ten weeks Germany launched its largest air raid of the war (38 Gothas and three 'Giants') on the night of 19/20 May 1918, the Whitsun Bank Holiday. It proved to be the last. A Bristol Fighter of No. 39 Squadron picked up one of the Gothas just after midnight, flying north of Hainault at 10,000ft (3,000m).

The Brisfit flown by Lieutenant Anthony Arkell with Air Mechanic Albert Stagg as observer/gunner was about 1,000ft (300m) higher and dived to attack. Arkell, just 19 years old, brought the Bristol to a position about 200 yards (180m) behind the Gotha under its tail to allow Stagg to fire off half a drum. Arkell then 'zoomed up' and fired a long burst from his Vickers before dropping back down to allow Stagg to engage again. Arkell reported that the Gotha '… dived and did flat turns. I fired several bursts with Vickers gun.… All this time Gotha was firing back with tracer all round machine.'

Arkell then moved in closer, sitting under the Gotha's tail allowing Stagg to fire off two more drums of ammunition before he 'zoomed up again' and fired another long burst from his forward firing gun. Only now did the pilot realize that the two

aircraft had dropped 7,000ft (2,100m) since the combat began but he swung back under the Gotha's tail and as his altimeter showed just 1,500ft (450m) Stagg open fire once more. This time his bullets struck home and the starboard engine burst into flames **(1)**.

It was clear that the Gotha was going down. All three of the crew jumped to their deaths **(2)**. Searchers found the body of 27-year-old Hans Thiedke on an allotment in Brooks Avenue 'a good half a mile north east of the Gotha'. That of Paul Sapkowiak, also aged 27, landed in 'a ditch some 300 yards south of the aeroplane wreckage' and the body of the third crew member, 20-year-old Wilhelm Schulte, was discovered a quarter of a mile to the south 'in the next field on the bank of a ditch'. Arkell recalled that the Gotha 'did about one and a half turns of spin' before crashing and 'bursting into a sheet of flame' as nearby residents crowded into the streets to witness the final moments of the London raider **(3)**. The burning wreckage lay spread over 100 yards (90m) of open ground between Roman Road and Beckton Road on the outskirts of East Ham.

problem meant he was unable to check the descent and, having unloaded the bombs, he made an emergency landing; the captain, Leutnant Wilhelm Rist was killed. Anti-aircraft guns also shot down two Gothas off the coast but claims for a third went unconfirmed; one more crashed on landing as it returned to Belgium.

Quiet now returned to the skies over London. The city's population, now reassured by the very visible aerial response to this latest attack, steeled themselves for the next alarm and the defenders confidently waited for their next test. A week passed, then a month, two months then three, but the raiders did not return; in fact they never came again.

SUMMARY

For Brandenburg, losses on this Whitsun raid were high as the defences demonstrated increasing efficiency, but he still planned to continue raiding England. However, on 27 May 1918, the German Army launched an attack on the Aisne and both Bogohl 3 and Rfa 501 were committed to supporting the attack. Brandenburg planned two more raids in July 1918 but the OHL cancelled them. However, by August the powerful Elektron incendiary bomb, weighing only 1kg and able to be dropped in vast numbers, was now ready. Plans to unleash a fearsome firestorm on Paris and London were in place and, in September, with the war going against Germany, the OHL initially took the decision to launch the firebombs. The crews prepared for this desperate attack, bombs were loaded, then, at the very last minute, an order arrived cancelling the raid. Since June 1918, following agitation at home, British aircraft had carried out raids on German towns and cities. Now, recognizing the end of the war was near and fearing even greater reprisals against a German civilian population whose morale was already disintegrating, the OHL cancelled the order to unleash the firestorm. For London's civilian population the war was over.

The Gotha and 'Giant' raids on the London area resulted in 486 deaths and 1,432 injuries (plus one killed and two wounded during a raid by an Albatross C VII in May 1917). Across the rest of south-eastern England (principally Folkestone, Margate, Harwich, Southend, Ramsgate, Chatham, Sheerness and Dover) there were another 350 deaths and 557 injuries – a total of 837 killed and 1,991 injured by aeroplane attacks. The British defences lost 16 aircraft to enemy action and in crashes.

While Germany's plan to crush the morale of London's population failed, on two occasions raids caused fighting squadrons to be withdrawn from the Western Front and many high-performance aircraft were committed to Home Defence instead of boosting Allied aerial strength at the front; the raids also contributed to a reduction in munitions production at times. Guns, searchlights and manpower were also required to complete the defence system to combat these raids, remaining in place until the end of the war despite urgent demands for their redeployment elsewhere. Yet this came at a price for the crews of Bogohl 3: estimates show that 60 Gothas were lost, 24 shot down or missing and 36 destroyed or seriously damaged by crash-landings in Belgium. In addition two 'Giants' were lost in bad landings.

The air raids made one final contribution, one that proved extremely beneficial to Britain. They made the British Government acutely aware of the need for an in-depth aerial defence system. The need to realign the divergent paths taken by the RFC and RNAS led to the creation of the RAF in 1918 and,

The Home Defence system made rapid progress during World War I, as shown by this photograph of the operations room, with large plotting table, at Spring Gardens. By the end of the war this room was the hub of a sophisticated information network.

by September 1918, a sophisticated central operations room at Spring Gardens in central London was in operation. Here was the hub of an exclusive military telephone network that relayed information from 25 sub-control centres, each in direct contact with the AA gun batteries, searchlight companies, balloon aprons, aerodromes and observer posts in its own area. Information from the sub-commands was fed via telephone headsets to a team of plotters working on a large map table, who moved symbols representing enemy aircraft across the map, all overseen from a gallery above by Ashmore, Higgins and a senior police representative. Ashmore was able to speak directly to the sub-commanders and Higgins to the fighter wing HQs, while the police representative had direct lines to the police and fire services. According to Ashmore, the system worked very well: 'From the time the observer at one of the stations in the country saw a machine over him, to the time when the counter representing it appeared on my map, was not, as a rule, more than half a minute.'

It was in essence the system that, with the addition of Radar, provided the country with its defence against the Luftwaffe when German aircraft returned to British skies in 1940.

THE SITES TODAY

The battle-scarred pedestal of the sphinx today, still bearing the wounds it sustained over 90 years ago. A closer inspection shows damage to the sphinx too.

Much of London has changed since the Gotha and 'Giant' raids of 1917–18. The destruction caused by the Blitz of 1940–41, the V1 and V2 rockets of 1944–45, as well as the subsequent and ongoing redevelopment of London, has seen roads and buildings disappear from great tracts of the city, but there are still a few reminders that link us with this turbulent time in the city's history.

A memorial in Poplar Recreation Ground, East India Dock Road, commemorates the deaths of 18 young schoolchildren killed while attending the Upper North Street School, Poplar, when the first Gotha daylight raid took place on 13 June 1917. Another reminder of that first bomber raid is a ceramic plaque in memory of PC Alfred Smith on the wall at Postman's Park (entrance in Aldersgate Street, EC1), who died while saving the lives of others. A unique memorial marking the second daylight raid on 7 July 1917, the twisted remains of a bomb that fell in Lombard Street, EC3, on the church of St Edmund the King and Martyr is now preserved in a glass case as an integral part of the altar.

In September the Gothas switched to night-time bombing and during the first moonlight raid on 4/5 September 1917 a bomb landed on the Victoria Embankment, a few feet from Cleopatra's Needle. The shrapnel wounds still scar the ancient obelisk, plinths and right-hand sphinx. The plaque on one of the plinths incorrectly refers to the raid as the 'first raid' on London by aeroplanes; it was the first night-time raid.

Later that month, on the night of 24 September, a bomb landed in the roadway in Southampton Row, WC2, outside the Bedford Hotel. The hotel has been completely rebuilt in the intervening years but a framed plaque outside remembers the 13 killed and 22 injured in the blast.

In Lincoln's Inn, outside 10 Stone's Buildings, there is a brass plaque commemorating a bomb that fell on 18 December 1917. A small white disc set in the tarmac marks the point where the bomb exploded and the walls of No. 10 show significant shrapnel damage. Finally, in Chelsea, a plaque on the wall of the north-east wing of the Royal Hospital commemorates its destruction by a 1,000kg bomb (incorrectly recorded on the plaque as a 500lb bomb) in February 1918, rebuilding in 1921, destruction again in 1945 by a V2 rocket and subsequent rebuilding in 1965.

ORDER OF BATTLE
FOR THE LONDON AIR RAIDS

13 JUNE 1917

Kampfgeschwader 3 der Oberste Heeresleitung (Kagohl 3)

20 Gothas – 2 returned early

Royal Naval Air Service (RNAS) – 33 aircraft

Dover: 3 x Sopwith Pup, 1 x Sopwith Baby

Eastchurch: 2 x Bristol Scout, 1 x Sopwith 1½ Strutter

Felixstowe: 2 x Sopwith Schneider, 5 x Sopwith Baby

Grain: 2 x Sopwith Pup, 2 x Sopwith Baby

Manston: 4 x Bristol Scout, 1 x Sopwith Pup, 2 x Sopwith Triplane

Westgate: 4 x Sopwith Baby

Walmer: 4 x Sopwith Pup

Royal Flying Corps (RFC) – 55 aircraft

No. 37 Squadron: 1 x BE2e, 1 x BE12, 1 x BE12a, 1 x RE7, 5 x Sopwith 1½ Strutter

No. 39 Squadron: 1 x BE2c, 2 x BE2e, 3 x BE12, 3 x BE12a, 1 x FK8

No. 50 Squadron: 1 x BE2c, 1 x BE12, 2 x BE12a, 5 x FK8, 1 x RE8, 1 x Vickers ES1

No. 65 Squadron: 2 x DH5

No. 78 Squadron: 1 x BE12a

No. 98 Depot Squadron (DS): 1 x BE2d, 1 x BE2e, 1 x BE12a

No. 35 Training Squadron (TS): 2 x Bristol Fighter

No. 40 TS: 2 x Sopwith Pup

No. 62 TS: 1 x Sopwith Pup

No. 63 TS: 1 x Sopwith Pup

No. 2 Aircraft Acceptance Park (AAP): 2 x DH4, 1 x DH5

No. 8 AAP: 1 x DH4, 1 x DH5, 1 x FE8, 1 x Sopwith 1½ Strutter, 1 x Bristol Fighter, 1 x RE8

Orfordness Experimental Station: 2 x Sopwith Triplane, 2 x DH4

7 JULY 1917

Kagohl 3

24 Gothas – 2 returned early

RNAS – 22 aircraft

Dover: 1 x Sopwith Pup, 2 x Sopwith Baby

Eastchurch: 2 x Sopwith Camel

Grain: 1 x Sopwith Pup

Manston: 1 x Sopwith Pup, 3 x Sopwith Camel, 4 x Sopwith Triplane, 3 x Bristol Scout

Walmer: 5 x Sopwith Pup

RFC – 78 aircraft

No. 37 Squadron: 2 x BE12, 3 x BE12a, 1 x BE2e, 1 x RE7, 4 x Sopwith Pup, 5 x Sopwith 1½ Strutter

No. 39 Squadron: 3 x BE12, 3 x BE12a, 2 x SE5, 1 x FK8

No. 50 Squadron: 2 x BE12a, 6 x Sopwith Pup, 1 x FK8, 1 x Vickers ES1, 3 x unrecorded aircraft

No. 78 Squadron: 5 x BE12a

No. 35 TS: 2 x Bristol Fighter

No. 40 TS: 1 x Sopwith Pup, 2 x unrecorded aircraft

No. 56 TS: 1 x Spad

No. 62 TS: 1 x Sopwith Pup

No. 63 TS: 2 x Sopwith Pup

No. 198 DS: 1 x Vickers FB12c

No. 2 AAP: 5 x DH4, 1 x DH5

No. 7 AAP: 1 x FE8

No. 8 AAP: 3 x Bristol Fighter, 1 x FE2d, 2 x FE8, 1 x DH5, 1 x FK8

Orfordness Experimental Station: 1 x Bristol Fighter, 1 x Sopwith Triplane, 1 x DH2, 1 x FE2b, 1 x Sopwith 1½ Strutter, 1 x FK8, 1 x RE8

Martlesham Heath Testing Squadron: 2 x Sopwith Camel, 1 x DH4

4/5 SEPTEMBER 1917

Kagohl 3

11 Gothas – 2 returned early

RFC – 18 aircraft

No. 37 Squadron: 1 x BE2d, 3 x BE2e, 1 x BE12a

No. 39 Squadron: 3 x BE2e, 3 x BE12

No. 44 Squadron: 4 x Sopwith Camel

No. 50 Squadron: 2 x BE12, 1 x FK8

24 SEPTEMBER 1917

Kagohl 3

16 Gothas – 3 returned early

RFC – 30 aircraft

No. 37 Squadron: 4 x BE2e, 2 x BE12

No. 39 Squadron: 4 x BE2e (inc. one W/T tracker aircraft), 1 x BE12, 1 x BE12a

No. 44 Squadron: 3 x Sopwith Camel

No. 50 Squadron: 5 x BE12 (three W/T tracker aircraft), 1 x BE2e, 2 x FK8

No. 78 Squadron: 2 x FE2d, 2 x Sopwith 1½ Strutter

Orfordness Experimental Station: 3 x unrecorded aircraft

25 SEPTEMBER 1917

Kagohl 3

15 Gothas – 1 returned early

RNAS – 2 aircraft

Manston: 2 x BE2c

RFC – 18 aircraft

No. 37 Squadron: 1 x BE2d, 2 x BE2e, 1 x BE12

No. 39 Squadron: 4 x BE2e (one W/T tracker aircraft), 1 x BE2c, 1 x BE12a

No. 44 Squadron: 3 x Sopwith Camel

No. 50 Squadron: 1 x BE2e

No. 78 Squadron: 1 x FE2d, 3 x Sopwith 1½ Strutter

29 SEPTEMBER 1917

Kagohl 3

7 Gothas – 3 returned early

Riesenflugzeugabteilung 501 (Rfa 501)

3 Giants – 0 returned early

RNAS – 3 aircraft

Manston: 3 x BE2c

RFC – 28 aircraft

No. 39 Squadron: 2 x BE2c, 6 x BE2e, 2 x BE12 (both W/T tracker aircraft), 1 x BE12a

No. 44 Squadron: 4 x Sopwith Camel

No. 50 Squadron: 4 x BE12, 3 x BE2e, 1 x FK8

No. 78 Squadron: 1 x FE2d, 3 x Sopwith 1½ Strutter

Orfordness Experimental Station: 1 x Martinsyde F1

30 SEPTEMBER 1917

Kagohl 3

11 Gothas – 1 returned early

RNAS – 2 aircraft

Manston: 2 x BE2c

RFC – 31 aircraft

No. 37 Squadron: 4 x BE2e (one W/T tracker)

No. 39 Squadron: 4 x BE2e (two W/T trackers), 2 x BE12, 1 x BE12a

No. 44 Squadron: 8 x Sopwith Camel

No. 50 Squadron: 1 x BE2e, 2 x BE12 (one W/T tracker), 2 x FK8

No. 78 Squadron: 1 x FE2d, 5 x Sopwith 1½ Strutter

Orfordness Experimental Station: 1 x Martinsyde F1

1 OCTOBER 1917

Kagohl 3

18 Gothas – 6 returned early

RFC – 18 aircraft

No. 37 Squadron: 1 x BE2e, 1 x BE12

No. 39 Squadron: 2 x BE2e, 2 x BE12a

No. 44 Squadron: 7 x Sopwith Camel

No. 78 Squadron: 1 x FE2d, 4 x Sopwith 1½ Strutter

31 OCTOBER/1 NOVEMBER 1917

Kagohl 3

22 Gothas – 0 returned early

RNAS – 5 aircraft

Eastchurch: 2 x Sopwith 1½ Strutter

Manston: 2 x Sopwith 1½ Strutter, 1 x DH4

RFC – 45 aircraft

No. 37 Squadron: 6 x BE2e (one W/T tracker)

No. 39 Squadron: 5 x BE2e, 3 x BE12 (one W/T tracker)

No. 44 Squadron: 13 x Sopwith Camel

No. 50 Squadron: 3 x BE12 (two W/T trackers), 1 x BE12a, 4 x FK8, 1 x BE2e

No. 78 Squadron: 6 x Sopwith 1½ Strutter, 3 x Sopwith 1½ Strutter SS (single-seater conversion)

6 DECEMBER 1917

Kagohl 3 – now redesignated Bombengeschwader 3 der OHL (Bogohl 3)

19 Gothas – 3 returned early

Rfa 501

2 Giants – 0 returned early

RFC – 32 aircraft

No. 37 Squadron: 1 x BE2d, 6 x BE2e, 1 x BE12

No. 39 Squadron: 2 x BE2e, 2 x Bristol Fighter, 3 x BE12

No. 44 Squadron: 6 x Sopwith Camel

No. 50 Squadron: 3 x BE12 (all W/T trackers), 4 x FK8

No. 78 Squadron: 4 x Sopwith 1½ Strutter SS

18 DECEMBER 1917

Bogohl 3

15 Gothas – 2 returned early

Rfa 501

1 Giant – 0 returned early

RFC – 46 aircraft

No. 37 Squadron: 3 x BE2e, 1 x BE12, 2 x BE12b

No. 39 Squadron: 2 x BE2e, 4 x Bristol Fighter

No. 44 Squadron: 8 x Sopwith Camel

No. 50 Squadron: 3 x BE12, 6 x FK8

No. 61 Squadron: 4 x SE5a

No. 78 Squadron: 9 x Sopwith 1½ Strutter SS, 1 x Sopwith 1½ Strutter, 1 x BE2e (W/T tracker), 2 x BE12

28/29 JANUARY 1918

Bogohl 3

13 Gothas – 6 returned early

Rfa 501

2 Giants – 1 returned early

RNAS – 6 aircraft

Dover: 4 x Sopwith Camel, 1 x Sopwith 1½ Strutter

Eastchurch: 1 x Sopwith Camel

RFC – Detailed returns not available

No. 37 Squadron: 15 sorties flown

No. 39 Squadron: 10 sorties flown

No. 44 Squadron: 25 sorties flown

No. 50 Squadron: 11 sorties flown

No. 61 Squadron: 9 sorties flown

No. 75 Squadron: 5 sorties flown

No. 78 Squadron: 22 sorties flown

29/30 JANUARY 1918

Rfa 501

4 Giants – 1 returned early

RNAS – 7 aircraft

Dover: 4 x Sopwith Camel, 1 x Sopwith 1½ Strutter

Walmer: 2 x Sopwith Camel

RFC – 69 aircraft

No. 37 Squadron: 3 x BE2e, 3 x BE12, 3 x BE12b

No. 39 Squadron: 8 x Bristol Fighter (one W/T tracker), 1 x BE2e (W/T tracker)

No. 44 Squadron: 15 x Sopwith Camel

No. 50 Squadron: 3 x BE12 (inc. one W/T tracker), 4 x BE12b (one W/T tracker), 5 x FK8

No. 61 Squadron: 7 x SE5a

No. 75 Squadron: 1 x BE2e, 1 x BE12, 1 x BE12b

No. 78 Squadron: 6 x Sopwith Camel, 3 x Sopwith 1½ Strutter SS, 3 x BE12, 1 x BE12a, 1 x BE12b

16 FEBRUARY 1918

Rfa 501

5 Giants – 1 returned early

RFC – 56 aircraft

No. 37 Squadron: 1 x BE2d, 5 x BE2e, 3 x BE12, 1 x BE12a

No. 39 Squadron: 7 x Bristol Fighter

No. 44 Squadron: 12 x Sopwith Camel

No. 50 Squadron: 3 x BE12 (one W/T tracker), 3 x BE12b (one W/T tracker)

No. 61 Squadron: 7 x SE5a

No. 78 Squadron: 7 x Sopwith Camel, 1 x Sopwith 1½ Strutter SS

No. 141 Squadron: 4 x BE12 (one W/T tracker)

No. 143 Squadron: 2 x FK8

17 FEBRUARY 1918

Rfa 501

1 Giant – 0 returned early

RFC – 66 aircraft

No. 37 Squadron: 5 x BE2e, 3 x BE12 (one W/T tracker), 4 x BE12b

No. 39 Squadron: 7 x Bristol Fighter

No. 44 Squadron: 12 x Sopwith Camel

No. 50 Squadron: 2 x BE2e, 4 x BE12 (two W/T trackers), 1 x BE12a, 1 x BE12b

No. 61 Squadron: 8 x SE5a

No. 78 Squadron: 9 x Sopwith Camel, 1 x Sopwith 1½ Strutter SS

No. 141 Squadron: 4 x BE12, 1 x BE12b

No. 143 Squadron: 4 x FK8

7/8 MARCH 1918

Rfa 501

6 Giants – 1 returned early

RFC – 41 aircraft

No. 37 Squadron: 2 x BE2e, 2 x BE12, 3 x BE12b

No. 39 Squadron: 8 x Bristol Fighter

No. 44 Squadron: 4 x Sopwith Camel

No. 50 Squadron: 3 x BE12 (two W/T trackers), 3 x BE12b

No. 61 Squadron: 6 x SE5a

No. 78 Squadron: 3 x Sopwith Camel

No. 112 Squadron: 1 x Sopwith Camel

No. 141 Squadron: 3 x BE12

No. 143 Squadron: 3 x FK8

19/20 MAY 1918

Bogohl 3

38 Gothas – 10 returned early

Rfa 501

3 Giants – 0 returned early

RAF – 86 aircraft

No. 37 Squadron: 5 x BE12, 2 x BE12a, 2 x BE12b, 1 x SE5a

No. 39 Squadron: 8 x Bristol Fighter (one W/T tracker)

No. 44 Squadron: 11 x Sopwith Camel

No. 50 Squadron: 1 x BE12 (W/T tracker), 1 x BE12b (W/T tracker), 7 x SE5a

No. 61 Squadron: 9 x SE5a

No. 78 Squadron: 10 x Sopwith Camel

No. 112 Squadron: 12 x Sopwith Camel

No. 141 Squadron: 7 x Bristol Fighter

No. 143 Squadron: 10 x SE5a

FURTHER READING

Castle, H. G., *Fire Over England* (London, 1982)

Castle, I., *Campaign 193: London 1914–17: The Zeppelin Menace* (Oxford, 2008)

Cole, C., and Cheesman, E. F., *The Air Defence of Britain, 1914–1918* (London, 1984)

Fegan, T., *The 'Baby Killers' – German Air Raids on Britain in the First World War* (Barnsley, 2002)

Fredette, Major R. H., *The First Battle of Britain 1917–1918* (London, 1966)

Hanson. N., *First Blitz* (London, 2008)

Hyde, A. P., *The First Blitz* (Barnsley, 2002)

Jones, H. A., *The War In The Air, vol. 5* (London, 1935)

Morris, J., *German Air Raids on Britain 1914–1918* (reprinted 1993)

Rawlinson, A., *The Defence of London, 1915–1918* (London, 1923)

White, C. M., *The Gotha Summer* (London, 1986)

INDEX

References to illustrations are shown in **bold**.